Social History
Assessment

To my own family, especially the Bowers, Traegers, and Andrews, whose history has empowered me to explore the past, appreciate the present, anticipate the future with hope

Social History
Assessment

Arlene Bowers Andrews
University of South Carolina

SAGE Publications
Thousand Oaks ■ London ■ New Delhi

For information:

Sage Publications, Inc.
2455 Teller Road
Thousand Oaks, California 91320
E-mail: order@sagepub.com

Sage Publications Ltd.
1 Oliver's Yard
55 City Road
London EC1Y 1SP
United Kingdom

Sage Publications India Pvt. Ltd.
B-42, Panchsheel Enclave
Post Box 4109
New Delhi 110 017 India

Printed in the United States of America

Library of Congress Cataloging-in-Publication Data

Andrews, Arlene Bowers.
Social history assessment / Arlene Bowers Andrews.
    p. cm.
Includes bibliographical references and index.
ISBN 1-4129-1413-2 or 978-1-4129-1413-0 (pbk. : alk. paper)
    1. Interviewing in psychiatry. 2. Medical history taking. 3. Outcome assessment (Medical care) 4. Mental health services—Research—Methodology. I. Title. [DNLM: 1. Interview, Psychological—methods. 2. Medical History Taking—methods. 3. Socioeconomic Factors. WM 141 A565s 2007]

RC480.7.A532 2007
616.89'075—dc22   2006021555

This book is printed on acid-free paper.

06 07 08 09 10   10 9 8 7 6 5 4 3 2 1

Acquisitions Editor:	Kassie Graves
Editorial Assistant:	Veronica Novak
Production Editor:	Kate Peterson
Copy Editor:	Kristin Bergstad
Typesetter/Designer:	C&M Digitals (P) Ltd.
Indexer:	Kay Dusheck
Cover Designer:	Candice Harman

Contents

List of Figures

Preface

When I was an undergraduate psychology major at Duke University, I took a graduate course in psychiatric autobiography taught by a cultural anthropologist who was also trained as a psychiatrist. As class projects, I wrote papers on authors of children's books and compared information from their childhood biographies with themes in their fictional works. I also wrote my own autobiography in a journal and submitted it to the professor for comment. That was my first foray into the power of personal history.

Early in my training as a social worker and later, while working on my advanced degree in clinical-community psychology, I was coached to take meticulous social histories as a foundation for therapeutic intervention. I was fascinated by the seemingly infinite volume of information in any individual's life script and the power of history to repeat itself within and across linked lives. I put this training to work in my first jobs, starting at programs for people with mental retardation and moving on to be part of multidisciplinary teams programs for people with disabilities and then children's mental health treatment. Generally I was the one who researched and reported the social history as a part of developing a treatment plan. When I moved on to develop expertise in child abuse and neglect and domestic violence, the significance of the social history gained even greater meaning, because it formed the basis for predicting the personal safety of vulnerable family members.

I truly began to realize the value of a social history after a group of lawyers came to me and asked if I could help them explain a criminal defendant's life experiences to a court. They were representing a man who had never been convicted of a crime until one night when, under the influence of alcohol and a drug cocktail, he drove by a police officer who was issuing a traffic citation to a stranger, pulled a handgun from his glove compartment, and killed the officer. I knew little about criminal behavior, but as they told me the man's story, I realized I knew a lot about his history. He had suffered every form of childhood abuse and never received support or treatment for the lasting effects of the trauma. The history of his victimization intruded into his victim's life, generating a new history of victimization. I knew that somehow the study and disclosure of these histories could open opportunities for healing and safer futures.

In the role of expert witness, I am sometimes asked to review the court records of a defendant who has been sentenced to die. In these records, I examine the testimony of social workers and other mental health professionals who presented trial testimony regarding the defendant's social history. Too often, I have left my desk after a court transcript review with grave concern, aware that the apparent skill of the prior witness is sorely lacking, because facts of the history, their interpretation, and the expert opinion have been so superficially offered to the court. Also, as I conduct forensic social history assessments, I am struck by the many missed "prevention points" throughout the defendant's history—those opportunities when professionals and members of the natural support system could have intervened in a way that would have significantly altered the sad trajectory of the person's history.

And so I felt compelled to write this book for professionals of multiple disciplines that rely on social histories. This includes those who conduct social history assessments—such as social workers, psychologists, counselors, nurses, psychiatrists, and other helping professionals—and those who use them—such as judges, lawyers, historians, biographers, and human service case managers. My experience is with social history assessments in diverse settings, therefore I wrote the book for general use. The majority of my experience is with survivors of victimizing experiences, so most of my case examples are drawn from those populations.

I have tried to put a variety of resources at the professional's fingertips: summaries of theories about human social behavior, tips for gathering and interpreting histories, and tools for summarizing and communicating information. Those readers who are learning about social history assessment for the first time will need to grasp the whole content of the book, including Chapters 2 and 3, which cover essential theory for understanding the material in the remainder of the book. Readers with advanced human services professional education may be able to skim the two theory chapters and move on to the material about conducting the assessment.

The book is a resource for developing thorough and comprehensive histories, though it includes tools that are useful in situations such as managed care settings, where interventions are brief and the history needs to be done as quickly and concisely as possible. Learning to conduct thorough histories forms an excellent foundation for also conducting them succinctly with focus on major presenting concerns.

I owe special appreciation to the many people who taught me the profound value that an excellent social history assessment can have in determinations of life or death. I cannot name them all, but I particularly stand in awe of people like David Bruck, John Blume, Drucy Glass, Pamela Blume Leonard, Scharlotte Holdman, Kathy Wayland, and the thousands of others who have given their lives to helping people understand how life history influences human behavior for better and for worse. I am also grateful to the American Psychological Foundation Randy Gersen Memorial Fund, which awarded support for my work on this book.

1

The Significance of a Person's Social History

Most people seem compelled to reflect on their own lives and dabble with exploring their family trees, even their genealogies. People ponder how they came to be uniquely themselves while carrying the innate and acquired traits of those who came before them. They boast of their ancestors, avoid mention of them for shame, or wonder about the mystery of the unknown. In recent years, through the Internet, people have gained easy access to treasure stores of information about past generations, spawning renewed popular interest in family history.

Many people explore their life histories primarily for pleasure or enlightenment, but there comes a time for some people when they need to explore their history to promote personal growth or healing. When people develop personal or social problems or encounter barriers to desired development, their concern is typically with discomfort in the present and immediate future. They will find that when they go to a helping professional, giving at least a brief social history marks the start of most therapeutic interventions. Exploring the client's origins helps build rapport and lay the foundation for mutual client-professional assessment of the here and now and what can happen in the future. This book focuses on the development of the individual history in the context of the helping relationship so that together, the person and professional can develop a plan for future life enhancement.

The helping professions have a long tradition of reliance on social histories as a tool to promote healing and growth. In this book, "helping professionals" will refer to people from various disciplines who have specialized knowledge, certified skill through advanced education and/or licensure, and a code of ethics that guides interventions aimed at helping another person manage a life problem or make critical decisions. Helping professionals are found in such fields as counseling, education, law, medicine, ministry, nursing, psychiatry, psychology, and social work. Each profession has its own body of knowledge and skills, including traditions regarding the use of social histories. Though independent, the knowledge bases for the professions often overlap and most professionals have worked on interdisciplinary teams, producing transdisciplinary knowledge that crosses over professional boundaries. Taking a personal history is one of the key transdisciplinary practices.

Different theories that guide helping professionals in their practice emphasize the power of history to varying degrees. For example, psychoanalysts and narrative therapists regard personal history as pervasive, while behaviorists essentially look at old habits, without intensive review of how they developed, and focus on forming new habits to replace them. Professionals draw on a variety of theories, tending to emphasize some over others. Regardless of the professional's theoretical grounding, most people who seek help can communicate comfortably, though perhaps selectively, in the language of personal stories. Many people are fascinated by life histories and eagerly explore their own. The professional will help the person honor the gifts of the past, tenderly confront any agonies that originated there, and learn new ways to heal and grow for the future.

The helping professional's use of life history can be informed by the growing body of research about life history in the social and behavioral sciences. Researchers in such fields as anthropology, sociology, genetics, criminology, psychology, social work, education, journalism, and, of course, history, are among the many who have advanced knowledge about how to effectively gather, record, describe, and interpret life histories and narratives as a means to understanding human behavior in the broader environmental context (see, e.g., Atkinson, 1998; Bruner, 1986; Hatch & Wisniewski, 1995; Josselson & Lieblich, 1993, 1995). The research methods have included focused studies of individual lives as well as studies of mass populations over multiple generations using life course methods (see, e.g., Giele & Elder, 1998; Mortimer & Shanahan, 2003). The findings from these studies portray the powerful influence that meaning and context have on individual development and behavior. Many of the studies have contributed to the articulation of methods for gathering and interpreting information that ensures fidelity to the narrator's story. The findings and the methods are useful in professional practice.

Edward Bruner (1984) suggests that a person's life can be regarded as the "life lived" (what actually happened), the "life experienced" (meanings, images, feelings, thoughts of the person), and the "life as told" (the narrative as influenced by cultural conventions of storytelling, audience, and social context). The "life lived" can be recorded as a life event history that identifies milestones, critical incidents, or key decision points in a person's life. The "life lived" is based on relatively objective information that can be substantiated by records or consensus by other people who witnessed or observed the events. The event history becomes a chronological list of events with identification of who did what, when, and where.

The latter two ways of knowing the life are based in the subjective impressions of the informant. The "life experienced" gets expressed through the "life as told" as well as the person's art, behavioral patterns, emotional expressions, and other forms of communication. The life event history can be illustrated with notes about the person's experience or response to events, such as recalled emotional reactions to or images of key events. The "life as told" is the personal narrative with its unique content and form. The narrative, which tends to express the meaning that a person gives to events that happened, itself offers information about the person's life history.

People relate their own life narratives through the filter of their memories and interpretive meanings, thereby revealing much about who they are now as well as who they were and what they did. Anthropologists James Peacock and Dorothy Holland (1993) propose using the term *life-focused* to refer to the history that primarily addresses the factual events and subjective experiences of the subject (i.e., the "life lived" and "life experienced," using Bruner's typology). They suggest that alternatively, the "story-focused" approach emphasizes the narrative, with emphasis on how the subject structures the story and the process of telling the story. For example, the narrator may have a coherent story, one that integrates life experiences and reflected meaning, or an incoherent story with scattered themes and reflections. The narrator may emphasize certain themes and minimize others. "Story-focused" approaches assume the subject's culture affects beliefs, ideas, and traditions about how the narrative is expressed. How the subject tells the story reflects the meaning the subject has made of his or her life experiences. Both approaches, together and separately, have value in different contexts. This book will address how to capture information about life experiences while emphasizing the significance of the narrative and interpretations of the story.

Life stories are contextual. Goodson (1995) maintains that the analysis of a life story in its political and economic context over time makes it a life history. Each part of a story occurs in time, at a place or series of places, and within a culture. In addition, an individual's life story is linked to the life stories of people close to him or her. A social history can be conducted for an individual, dyad, family, small group, organization, or community.

Life stories are dynamic, emerging over time, even as they are told. The listener (e.g., the caseworker or therapist) becomes a part of the story. Life stories are also developmental, open to reinterpretation as the person gains new knowledge or insight. This is the key to the helping professional's intervention. Like any good historical research, the meaning of the social history emerges through skilled interpretation of the history, development of a subjective current understanding about the past, and application of this understanding to future action.

Helping professionals listen to people as they tell their stories, add their own interpretations to the story, and often supplement the personal narrative with other sources of information, such as the perspectives of others who know the person or records left by people who have known or interacted with the person. The professional's interpretations are grounded in knowledge and skill derived from theories, empirical studies, and experiences about how other humans have managed similar circumstances. Together the professional and client share their interpretations as they move through the change process. Skilled professionals carefully reflect on their own interpretations in order to distinguish them from their client's interpretations. The dual perspectives shed greater light on the patterns and features of a life history.

When people construct their own histories from their own impressions and their interpretations of what others have said to them orally or in records, they are essentially being autobiographical. When outsiders describe a life history, they are biographical, and can construct the history without even consulting the subject of the history, using information from others and records. This formerly happened often, for example, when children or older people with disabilities were assessed and their own perspectives were ignored, before their rights of self-determination and participation were asserted and affirmed by law and professional standards. The autobiographical and biographical perspectives each have value. By bringing them together, the social context of the individual's life can often be better understood. Given that life histories are socially constructed, they are constantly evolving, changing as the historian, be that self or other, develops fresh perspectives based on new life experiences. In the context of a relationship with a helping professional, the person can develop fresh ways of looking at new life experiences so that future historical constructions promote life enhancement.

The Focus on Social Relations

Humans are complex creatures. Their thoughts, emotions, behaviors, and sensations are affected by their biology, psychology, and social relations. This book particularly addresses the personal *social* history,[1] that is, the social relationships that have influenced the development of the person during the life course. The life history also includes the person's biological development, including normative health, wellness behaviors, and maturation as well as illnesses, disabilities, injuries, or behaviors detrimental to health. It also involves psychological development, including learning and performance ability, emotional and behavioral regulation, communication and information processing, personality and identity development, mental health, and the host of factors that make up the individual as a person. The term *biopsychosocial* was coined to refer to the holistic assessment of a personal history.

A thorough understanding of the social aspects of a life must be informed to some extent by the biological and psychological aspects of the life. This book therefore briefly addresses essential elements of biological and psychological assessment, but the emphasis is on *social* history. Social relations involve the association of self with others. All individuals are influenced by and exert influence on the people around them. From a developmental and social ecological perspective, a person's social relations grow more complex over time. They start in infancy with intimate relations between the infant and primary caregivers and extend to include less familiar people, such as teachers and other caregivers, peers, social acquaintances, neighbors, contacts in the community, and messengers brought by various media from the broader society and culture. Interactions with the social networks become integral to the person's evolving social history.

Social interactions powerfully influence human development. Each human is born with a unique genetic constitution and innate capacities. The extent to which many of these capacities are realized is elicited, from birth onward, through interactions with the external environment. That environment includes the physical world, with its temperature, light, sounds, smells, images, and other stimuli. It also includes, critically, the social environment, and the other humans who, if they are nurturing, link the infant and young child to food, water, protection, comfort, and modeling of developmentally appropriate human behavior. The infinite variety of external influences sends messages to the baby's growing brain and helps to shape its development. Even in utero, the developing fetus can be influenced by the mother's social situation to the extent that it affects her nutritional intake, health, stress level, and other conditions.

Understanding a person's social history and how the person makes meaning of the history is a key to helping the person relate socially in ways that are healthy and fulfilling.

The Social History: Overview

Social histories take many forms in the helping professions. In a managed care world, when a psychotherapist may have only six 55-minute sessions to assess a client and promote healthy bereavement and coping after a sudden divorce, the history may take only moments. At another extreme, when a person's life is at stake, as when a defendant faces a possible sentence of death from a court of law, the defense team will scour the earth in search of information and expert opinion about the social history to explain how the history affected the defendant at the time of the crime and mitigates a sentence of death. In either case, the skilled professional will follow a standard that elicits adequate information for the goals of the process with the client.

The social history is a time-honored practice, as reflected in this description by one of the founders of the social work profession, Mary Richmond, in 1917:

> Social diagnosis is the attempt to arrive at as exact a definition as possible of the social situation and personality of a given client. The gathering of evidence, or investigation, begins the process, the critical examination and comparison of evidence follows, and last come its interpretation and the definition of the social difficulty. (p. 62)

This series of steps still forms the fundamental process in a social history assessment. The assessment is often followed by a final stage—planning a course of action to change the problem. And, given a century of research and theory development regarding human behavior in the social environment, the process is grounded in theoretical frameworks that guide the professional's approach to the whole assessment.

This book follows the sequence of steps in a social history assessment, as follows:

The Professional Lens. Chapters 2 and 3 review core theories that guide professional understanding of human behavior in the social environment. Theory provides the interpretive paradigm that professionals can contribute to the relationship with the client as they make meaning of the social history. This step begins with the professional's training and experience prior to interacting with the client. Scores of theories from multiple disciplines guide various health and human services professionals; only a few core theories are covered here. Chapter 2 address fundamental themes in human social development through the life span: environmental context and social systems theory, the life course, and critical processes in social development. The discussion addresses barriers to and resources for prosocial and healthy development with a focus on the social functions of learning and adaptation, attachment and stability, stress and coping, and deprivation. Chapter 3 summarizes the social environment, including family, social network, and community influences on the development of individual behavior. The chapter closes with an examination of factors in the broad social environment, including culture, class, race-ethnicity, location, spirituality, and government and public policy.

The material in Chapters 2 and 3 is just the tip of an iceberg that is loaded with empirical and conceptual information available to helping professionals. The information will be familiar to people with advanced education in the social or behavioral sciences or professions. They might use the chapters as a ready reference guide or skip them altogether. For relative novices in the field of social history, the two chapters are critical to comprehending the interpretation phase of the social history assessment.

The individual life story becomes a speck in a universe of information about human behavior in the social environment. The life story can be deconstructed from a variety of perspectives. Individuals are the best informants and decision makers about which themes are most salient in their lives. As professionals listen carefully to how individuals express the themes in their social histories, the professional interpretation will enable a fresh perspective that can help the individual gain new insight.

Describing the Social History. Chapter 4 covers the gathering of facts and observations that lead to the description of the history and the recording of meaning that participants in the history have made of the life events. A description is essentially a straightforward reporting of what was detected by the professional and person as they made a record of the life history. The history description is grounded in information from multiple interviews, records and reports, and direct observation. The professional uses tools such as genograms, sociograms, chronology, time lines, and other aids to summarize the information. Chapter 4 essentially addresses how complex human experience can be summarized in ways that promote clarity and manageable focus on critical themes. The descriptive part of the history helps to differentiate effects of past from effects of life events in the here and now.

Making Meaning: Interpreting the Social History. Chapter 5 addresses the blending of theory, facts, and observations as the history is critically examined and interpreted. The social history assessment helps to explain how people function socially and how their histories have influenced the way they think, feel, and behave. The chapter reviews the analytic and synthesizing processes that are applied and presents a case study to illustrate the art of history interpretation in the human services. By achieving deeper understanding, the person or others connected to the person can make decisions about how to move forward into the future—thereby shaping their own history and contributing to the histories of those who come behind them.

The steps suggest a logical sequence, although chronologically each step may be revisited in a series of iterations. For example, as facts are gathered, the professional may consult specialized sources of information or theory to inform the interpretation. As interpretations take shape, additional facts may be gathered. As plans for future action are explored, meaning may be reinterpreted, and so on.

Tools to Aid Social History Development. Finally, Chapter 6 is a repository of standard tools used in social history data gathering, descriptions, and interpretations. The first is the extensive "Social History Interview Topical Guide," a list of factors to include during interviews. The "Sample Family Social History Assessment Instruments" summarizes several standardized instruments that are commonly used to gather social history assessments. The "Checklist for Social History Records Compilation" identifies the type of records that accumulate during a person's life and offers a list of Web-based resources for gathering genealogical information.

The chapter also includes classic tools to describe social relationships, including the genogram and sociogram (also known as ecomap). Examples are provided for tools that describe life events, including the chronology, life history calendar, and abbreviated time line. The chapter also discusses how figures such as maps, building plans, and community profiles can complement a social history.

These stages—professional theoretical grounding, describing the history with tools as necessary, and interpreting the history—form the essential steps in social history assessment. In addition, any professional practice must be grounded in solid mastery of ethical issues. Before examining ways to conduct social history assessments, a discussion of relevant ethical issues is in order.

Ethical Issues in Assessing Social History

"'What is real?' asked the rabbit one day."[2]

Helping professionals might ask the same as they listen to their clients' stories. A person's life story includes what really happened—that is, the truth of the matter—as well as the meaning the person makes of what happened. The telling of the story (the narrative) is constrained by language, images, or records of what happened. When listeners such as helping professionals hear the story or see evidence of what happened, they also make meaning about the story. So the process of telling, hearing, recording, and interpreting the life history in the context of a relationship with a helping professional requires careful attention if the reality of the situation is to be understood.

Life stories are revealed through multiple venues. People tell their own stories orally, in writing, through art, or with other media. Other people may talk or write about them. Records about a person are kept, such as when a teacher records grades, a nurse records health status, or a mother makes a scrapbook. The "truth" may be some objective reality that happened, but each person involved in the person's network interprets the reality and makes her or his own meaning from it. The interpretations are as important as the truth of the story.

Writing of narrative inquiry, Blumenfeld-Jones (1995) distinguished "truth" and "fidelity" by stipulating that truth is "what happened" and fidelity is "what it means to the teller of the tale" (p. 26). The professional who hears and possibly retells a person's story must apply fidelity from at least two perspectives. One has to do with being true to what the person said about the facts and the meaning he makes of the facts. The other has to do with being true to the context of the story even if the person does not articulate the context. For example, if a youth tells about an incident at school, the professional needs to interpret the story with some degree of understanding about the school within its cultural, community, and historical context. Practicing fidelity requires the professional to listen attentively to the unique perspectives of the client while exercising or acquiring cultural competence about the context.

When telling their stories, people may offer a description of their perceptions of truth, that is, what happened, that varies from what others describe as the truth. Denzin (1989) observed that a historically truthful statement is in accord with empirical data about the event or experience (p. 23). Truthful statements agree with how various people, in a "community of minds," describe what occurred or what they believe occurred.

The person's telling the facts of the life story, the way it is told, and the meaning are all critical to the helping relationship. With regard to the truth about the facts of the story, obtaining an honest, accurate, and complete life history promotes a more productive relationship between professional and client. Yet professionals must concede, as did Barone (1995), that "a life story never tells the absolute truth" (p. 64). A story can never be complete to the finest detail, even when the person tries hard to accurately and thoroughly recall facts.

Of course, people often choose to convey the facts through their own lens of meaning, which causes the facts to appear distorted or confusing. For example, a man and woman may share an experience that involves the man striking the woman. An objective observer might describe the act as the man's intentional use of his open hand against the woman's face. In telling the story, the man might say he did not strike her, that his hand brushed her face because he was trying to move her out of his way. The female victim might say the man aimed his hand at her and hit so quickly she did not have time to protect herself. Without an objective observer, who will the professional believe? The professional will rely on contextual knowledge, particularly awareness of research about interpersonal violence, which will suggest that the man will tend to tell the story in socially desirable ways to avoid shame and attempt to maintain a sense of control. Still, this awareness must be tempered by careful assessment of the stories using some of the techniques reviewed here. Perhaps the man is being honest.

While individual perceptions of truth may vary, other factors can also compound discernment of the truth. People may repeat family myths, those stories that have been passed from one generation to another that may have partial or no basis in fact but are believed by the family members. For example, some families pass on the idea that they are descended from royal families in places like Scotland, Rumania, or Egypt. They have no concrete basis for the belief, and in some cases research indicates this cannot be so, but the belief is empowering and would be hard to cast aside after generations of conviction. On a shorter time frame, a parent might relate a personal historical event in a way that it takes on mythical proportions, such as stories about how he or she survived hard times. Reference to help from family and friends gets omitted to emphasize the self-sufficiency and resilience of the parent under stress. Family myths are essential expressions of the family's perceptions of itself and thus should be valued.

People may withhold family secrets, guarding them carefully to minimize risk of painful emotional disruption. Outside the family system, families avoid mention of information about circumstances they regard as emotionally damaging or shameful, such as criminal acts, affairs, abuse, addiction, or conception out of wedlock. These secrets often exert powerful influence in the family dynamics. Helping professionals are trained to carefully and respectfully work with clients to discuss secrets. In many cases, secrets should be left alone and untold until the person and the family system are prepared to manage emotions and communication about the revelation.

While honoring people's myths and privacy, professionals may need to gather facts to understand what really happened in a life history. They can rely on a number of guides to discern whether the client is trying to tell the truth. A life story is *credible* when it convincingly conveys what happened and how the person felt about it. Helping professionals can draw from the lessons of credibility specialists in law, psychology, and criminal justice who dedicate their careers to the pursuit of truth, detection of lies, and establishment of credibility in witnesses for courts of law. They have developed criteria such as these for determining whether a witness is competent to testify (Myers, 1998):

- Adequate intelligence and memory
- Ability to perceive through various senses, recall, and communicate information
- Knowledge of the difference between truth and a lie
- Understanding of consequences of not telling the truth
- Understanding of the moral obligation in an oath to tell the truth

A person's credibility might be questioned if, for example, he or she has memory problems or a mental disturbance that blocks understanding of the difference between truth and fantasy.

When professionals seek to establish the truth about a social history, they must rely on the person who is the subject of the history and people who knew the subject well and were witnesses to his or her life. Even written records are documents produced by people who interacted with the subject. Questions of credibility may arise, particularly given that facts are often communicated along with opinions and feelings that may cause distortions or omissions of facts. For example, informants may deny, minimize, or exaggerate facts. Their tendency to do this contributes significant information to the interpretation of the history but clouds the professional's grasp of what really happened in the subject's life.

A story is more likely to be truthful if validity, reliability, and accuracy are high and bias is low. Validity is the extent to which the facts as reported fit the events as they actually occurred. Validity is more likely if the informant was a direct witness to the event and is not relaying information that was passed on from other sources. For example, a son tells his dad that his younger brother watched his mom go out the door and she left without a word, but the daughter says that she saw their mom as she left and that she was cheerfully smiling and said "Adios!" as she closed the door. The daughter's story is more valid because she actually saw the mother and the son is only relaying what he heard from the brother.

Validity is also more likely if the informant has no or little bias, that is, is unlikely to gain or lose anything by telling the story in a particular way. The telling is balanced and fair to all parties in the story. For example, a distraught mother says she observed her son in class and that his behavior was out of control. She wants him sent away to a residential school. The school psychologist was observing at the same time and noted the child was active but trying to pay attention. The professional's opinion has less bias.

Reliability is the consistency of reported facts over time or across observations. If multiple observers see the events in the same way, the story is more reliable than if they report the event differently. For example, when several adult children independently call their father a "tyrant" and give similar accounts of his abusive behavior, the information is more reliable than when one adult child says he was a "tyrant" and others present the stories in different ways, such as "he once got mean" or "he was all bark and no bite." A story is also more reliable if an individual reports the facts the same way at different points in time (i.e., the story does not change). Inconsistent or ambiguous information makes a story unreliable.

When professionals know the truth of a story, they can respond more helpfully to the way the person tells the story or makes meaning of it. If a client tells the life story in a way that is not truthful, that is information of use to the professional in understanding the client. Many people have good reason to falsify, minimize, or deny facts. Recall may provoke traumatic stress, guilt, or emotional overloads for which the client is unprepared. Minimizing helps to regulate emotions. This happens often with survivors of traumatic experiences such as rape or war combat. When clients are ready to deal with the emotions, the professional can encourage them to disclose the truth, ensuring them of their safety. The opposite may also occur when a client distorts the truth by telling the story with inflammatory remarks, extreme release of emotions, and embellishment of the facts. In other cases, the client may need to withhold truth to protect him- or herself or someone else. In rare cases, clients will try to deceive the professional and others for personal gain. Professionals can acquire advanced training to assess deception (Rogers, 1997). In any case, how the client discloses truth is an indicator of social functioning and is itself a part of the individual's social history.

The professional's communication skills can promote the client's honest and high quality narration of his or her story. A person who discloses a life history must have strong trust in the listener. The person has a right to feel safe and in control, especially with regard to what is disclosed. Trust is founded in mutual respect and the narrator's confidence that the listener will be committed to listening fully to the story. The narrator and listener should develop a rapport; this often begins as the listener takes the narrator through an informed consent procedure that explains the purpose of asking questions related to the history and shares information about the listener's qualifications to help the narrator interpret the history within their relationship. The listener must take care to maintain a nonjudgmental attitude.

Privacy and confidentiality are keys to maintaining trust. People reveal intensely personal and intimate experiences and feelings in their life stories. The narrator needs to know that the listener will protect the privacy of disclosed information and be assured that any records made will be maintained confidentially. Of course, the professional must disclose any exceptions to privacy, such as the legal requirement to report child abuse or elder abuse. In some cases, the client may be asked to waive privacy, as when the professional will offer testimony about a person's history in a court of law. Professionals should never push clients to reveal anything they are reluctant or unwilling to reveal. Every human's right to self-determination should be respected.

The person who shares his or her story should expect to benefit from the experience. In some cultures, revealing a story about oneself creates a special bond with the listener, who then assumes responsibility for protecting the story and the person. In a helping relationship, the person can gain fresh perspectives on his or her life through the knowledge and wisdom of the professional. But the telling of the story may elicit painful memories or have other negative effects. Such events create opportunities for healing if the professional is skilled in facilitating the client's interpretation of the feelings and adoption of healthy ways to cope.

What people choose to say depends on why they are saying it. Most clients voluntarily share their stories for many purposes. For example, they may be searching for a way to understand a disability, reduce anxiety, or make a major life decision. They will offer the information that seems to be most relevant to the purpose of the telling. In other cases, the involuntary client must tell the story or face negative consequences, as when a child protective service worker interviews a parent accused of child neglect. The involuntary client will be motivated to present biased information, particularly that which is favorable, so the helping professional is likely to look to other sources for information about the facts of the situation, such as other people who know the situation or records about it.

The professional and client must decide how much detail is necessary for the purposes of their work together. Telling a life story can take hours, days, weeks, even years. The professional may use a free-form approach to gathering information that encourages the client to tell the story in his or her own way, with as much detail and at a pace that is comfortable for the client. Or the professional may use any number of tools such as interview protocols, standardized assessments, or logs to focus the collection of information and expedite the process. The professional may take the history only from the informant or also rely on "collateral contacts," people who know the person well and can share their own perspectives on the person's life history. This is often done in the case of children or people with communication disabilities, such as those with intellectual impairments or frailties of old age. The primary caregiver, spouse, siblings, teacher, or other social network members can contribute to the history development.

A life history is *coherent* if it all fits together. That is, the facts, the way the story is told, and the client's expression of meaning are understandable given the contexts in which the life occurred and the story is narrated. The professional can enhance the coherence by triangulation. In research, triangulation involves using two or more theories, data sources, methods, or investigators to study a single phenomenon and converge on a single construct (Creswell, 2002). The term comes from navigational tools that use two visible points to plot the location of a third point. Triangulation can occur by collecting data at different points in time, at different sites, from different people or groups, or with different data collection procedures (e.g., interview and review of records) or data analysis techniques. If the sources all indicate the same phenomenon, then it is more likely to be true. When researching a life history, care must be taken to ensure that sources of information are in fact independent. For example, if a teacher's notes, mother, and sibling all say "mother says he fell on his head," then there is really only one source—the mother.

The professional has an ethical responsibility to help put the client's story together in a way that promotes truth and fidelity. Returning to the example of the man who struck the woman, the helping professional is likely to ponder these questions while working to discern whose story is closer to the truth: Who is more credible? Why? Which story is more valid? Who is the more reliable informant? Does the person trust me enough to tell the full truth? Will any benefit or harm come from telling the truth? Will it lead to violations of privacy? What purpose does each version of the story serve? Is this story coherent?

The personal social history is told in many ways. Ideally, the truth of the story emerges with fidelity to the meaning the client has made of the story. As professionals listen, record, and interpret the story, they must take care to maintain fidelity to the client's perspective on the story. Professional ethics codes promote the search for truth and the avoidance of participation in deception. For example, psychologists seek to promote accuracy, honesty, and truthfulness (American Psychological Association [APA], 2003, Principle 3, "Integrity"). Similarly, "Social workers should not participate in, condone, or be associated with dishonesty, fraud, or deception" (National Association of Social Workers [NASW], 1999, Principle 4.04, Dishonesty, Fraud, and Deception). The professional must take care to avoid listening selectively or retelling the story with inaccuracies. The client deserves to trust that the professional "gets it."

Ethically, the helping professional will strive to learn and understand the truth and the client's meaning as accurately and thoroughly as possible. Professionals can lend their own training and understanding to interpreting the client's life story. This will be informed by the professional's knowledge of theories and research findings regarding topics of relevance to the client's life, such as the information covered in Chapters 2 and 3 of this book. Even though the published theories and research emerge after rigorous scientific procedures and expert peer review to promote accuracy and valid representation of real world phenomena, they are subject to criticism because they are culturally and historically bound, affected by the theorist's or researcher's biases, and based on conclusions drawn from studies with methodological limits. The professional brings knowledge and practice wisdom to the helping relationship, but must do so humbly and with utmost regard for fidelity to the client's unique life. Any retelling of the story must be truthful, clear, and fair.

Unfortunately, I have observed health and human services workers who sometimes regard the social history as a simple checklist of information believed to be true, minimizing the significance of finding the truth or interpreting the history. This makes the history simply a life story from the informant's perspective. In professional practice, a social history *assessment* goes beyond recording the facts and applies professional wisdom, together with the client's meaning, to understanding the social life of the person.

Conducting a social history assessment can be an intensely emotional experience. People share their greatest joys and deepest sorrows, pride and shame, desires and burdens. Often, after sharing their stories with a caring, reflective professional, clients comment, "I've never told anyone that before" or "I've never thought of it that way before." They express new understanding about their personal experiences within the social world. They go forward into the future with fresh perspectives on how their histories have shaped their lives and how they can shape what will become their histories.

Notes

1. Historians use the term *social history* to refer to history that addresses the social aspects of a society or community, such as domestic relations or faith practices. In the helping professions, "social history" refers to the social life experiences of an individual.

2. Margery Williams, 1958, *The Velveteen Rabbit*, p. 1. New York: Doubleday.

2

The Professional Lens, Part I

Human Social Development and the Life Course

Human social behavior emerges from complex determinants. Humans are born with innate traits and potential capabilities. As they develop, they learn to behave within social contexts that encourage and limit their range of behaviors (Anderson & Sabatelli, 1999). From an early age, they learn the range of behaviors that are considered acceptable in their various environments, all the while making their own contributions to the nature of the environments in which they exist. Social context is based in time and place with social norms and forces that affect how people think, feel, act, and relate to one another. Within any social context, what people choose to do is based on their own capabilities, beliefs about themselves and the situation, and facilitating and inhibiting factors in the context.

This chapter and the next review basic knowledge and theory about how humans develop social behaviors. The overarching frameworks come from the fields of developmental science, with focus on individuals and families, and social ecology, which explains how social environmental factors influence the individual across the life span.

Human Development and the Life Course

Human life is bounded by time. Change through time is the nature of human existence. Humans develop throughout their lives, changing physiologically, intellectually, emotionally, socially, and in other ways. Although each individual is unique, some developmental changes occur in predictable sequences, such as walking, talking, starting school, puberty, moving away from home, or retiring from work. These are known as milestones. Other developmental changes occur in response to less predictable life experiences, such as accidents, job loss, untimely death of a child, or divorce. As people move through their lives, they must adapt to the milestones and experiences. How they adapt will affect their well-being positively or negatively.

Developmental Processes

This chapter focuses on child development because it lays the foundation for subsequent development throughout life. Early experiences do not automatically foretell later life conditions, though. Humans are highly malleable—until the day of death, humans adapt, changing continually as each day brings new learning. Their chances of adapting in socially healthy ways are increased if they have a healthy foundation in early childhood.

The human pace of development progresses more rapidly in the first 3 years than at any other time. The U.S. National Academy of Sciences convened a panel of experts, the Committee on Integrating the Science of Early Childhood Development, that reviewed the science of early development and identified these principles that guide the developmental process (Shonkoff & Phillips, 2000):

1. Human development is shaped by a dynamic and continuous interaction between biology and experience.

2. Culture influences every aspect of human development and is reflected in childrearing beliefs and practices designed to promote healthy adaptation.

3. The growth of self-regulation is a cornerstone of early childhood development that cuts across all domains of behavior.

4. Children are active participants in their own development, reflecting the intrinsic human drive to explore and master one's environment.

5. Human relationships are the building blocks of healthy development.

6. The broad range of individual differences among young children often makes it difficult to distinguish normal variations and

maturational delays from transient disorders and persistent impairments.

7. The development of children unfolds along individual pathways whose trajectories are characterized by continuities and discontinuities, as well as by a series of significant transitions. For example, increasing memory functions are gradual and continuous. A developmental transition involves an enduring reorientation in how the child relates to the environment, as in beginning to use language.

8. Human development is shaped by the ongoing interplay between sources of vulnerability and sources of resilience. Vulnerability can lead to poor outcomes; resilience promotes well-being.

9. The timing of early experiences can matter, but, more often than not, the developing child remains vulnerable to risks and open to protective influences throughout the early years of life and into adulthood.

10. The course of development can be altered in early childhood by effective interventions that change the balance between risk and protection, thereby shifting the odds in favor of more adaptive outcomes.

The panel agreed that humans are born wired for feelings and ready to learn and that nurturing environments are essential for healthy development.

Developmental Domains

The United Nations, through the *Convention on the Rights of the Child (CRC)*, provides a holistic framework for human development that stipulates that the human has the right to develop in five ways (Andrews & Kaufman, 1999):

1. *Physical development* includes wellness, disease or disability management, and exercise of physical abilities. A child needs support to attain an adequate standard of health, including the provision of nutritious food and clean drinking water, protection from harm, protection from environmental pollution, and access to health care services. A child with physical or mental disabilities,

according to the UN *CRC,* has a right to a full and decent life and special care.

2. *Mental development* includes realization of cognitive potential as well as emotional stability and mental health. The *Preamble* to the UN *CRC* recognizes that the child should grow up in a family environment, in an atmosphere of happiness, love, and understanding, suggesting that a child's emotional health should be promoted. Children need a clear sense of identity, including knowledge about family of origin on the mother and father's sides of the family. They have a right to education, which in the United States is increasingly taken from children through expulsion policies, and access to secondary and higher education. Children need protection from exposure to harm that could induce mental problems, including illicit drug use and trafficking, sexual exploitation, inhumane discipline, and all forms of maltreatment. When they are traumatized, they are entitled to measures to promote physical and psychological recovery for child victims of maltreatment and other trauma. Children with mental disabilities are entitled to special care.

3. *Spiritual development* enables children to appreciate themselves in a broader context and to understand spiritual and religious matters. Article 14 of the UN *CRC* asserts the child's right to freedom of thought, conscience, and religion and requires states to respect the duties and rights of parents in directing the child to exercise this right in a manner consistent with the evolving capacities of the child. Article 30 supplements this right by prohibiting the denial of the child's right to enjoy his or her own ethnic, religious, or linguistic minority culture or indigenous community.

4. *Moral development* facilitates responsible behavior and value-based belief systems. Children should be taught to respect one another's rights and be prepared for societal responsibility and cooperative, tolerant lives among diverse populations. When children are alleged or found to have behaved irresponsibly by breaking the law, they should be treated in a way that promotes the child's sense of dignity and worth and reinforces the child's respect for the human rights and fundamental freedoms of others, thus promoting the child's moral development.

5. *Social development* promotes healthy and productive connections among the child and other people. References to parents, family,

others responsible for the child, group affiliations, culture, and community permeate the *CRC*. The child's rights to developmentally appropriate social activities such as leisure and play, art and cultural life, and work are protected. The child should be protected from work that may be harmful to the child's health or physical, mental, spiritual, moral, or social development. Children should be encouraged to form social groups through freedom of association and peaceful assembly. The child's discovery of how to balance the critical relation of self-interest and the interests of others is the key to healthy social behavior and discouragement of antisocial behavior.

The *Convention on the Rights of the Child* recognizes the child's parents and family as primarily responsible for securing living conditions to meet the developmental needs, and it also designates nation states as responsible for providing material assistance and supporting parents in their responsibilities. This assistance and support generally is provided through transfer programs and community resources. Children can suffer deprivation when their communities or states fail to provide essential support.

Although the *CRC* focuses on the young human, the five developmental domains provide a holistic way of looking at human development through adulthood, too.

Expectations for Healthy Development in the United States

Expectations regarding human development vary from one culture to another. In the United States, members of society are expected to acquire an education—preferably high school or beyond—become economically self-sufficient, pay taxes for the common good, conform to civil and criminal laws, and hopefully contribute constructively to civil society. Members who have special needs are cared for by their families with support from schools, health care providers, and the nonprofit sector. Generally, state policy assumes exceptions to these conditions are temporary or unusual and, through eligibility determination, provides limited residual intervention such as economic assistance, child protection, or institutionalization.

Various studies indicate that in the United States positive child development, as evidenced by academic achievement, social adjustment, and physical health (Amato, 1995; Bronfenbrenner, 2005b; Hamburg, 1996; Shonkoff & Phillips, 2000), is associated with the following:

- adequate nourishment
- dependable attachments to parents or other adult caregivers
- adult-child nurturing interaction through holding, touching, smiling, talking
- available, responsive, consistent caregiver behavior in response to the child
- protection from physical and psychological harm
- cognitively stimulating physical and social environment
- firm, consistent, flexible discipline strategies
- social support and guidance when faced with adversity
- play activities and opportunities to explore
- more than one consistently involved adult who provides economic resources, support, regulation, and positive role modeling to the child

Material resources such as nutritious food, safe water, clothing, and housing are necessary but insufficient for holistic development. Stable, nurturing social relationships and safe, stimulating environments are also essential.

The transition period from childhood to adulthood can be difficult. It involves such developmental tasks as

- self-definition
- developing a personal set of values
- problem solving and decision making appropriate for adult roles
- social skills for interaction with parents, peers, and others
- emotional independence from parents
- ability to negotiate the pressure from and acceptance of peers
- experimentation with a range of behaviors, attitudes, and activities (see Furstenberg, Eccles, & Cook, 1999)

When a young person's developmental progress is hindered and negative socialization has occurred the results can be disastrous, including aggression toward parents or others.

After young adults are "launched" and out of their parental homes, they tend to develop relatively stable traits while continuing to adapt to new experiences. Predictable transitions include entering a career, mating, and parenthood. These do not necessarily occur in that order. For example, parenthood often occurs before teens or young adults leave their own homes of origin. Furthermore, developmental trajectories may be marked by multiple changes. The once-predictable school-to-work sequence is now more likely to be school, work, more school, different work, and so on. People change careers and often change mates as well. Increasing life expectancy means more families have multiple older generations—with grandparents, great-grands, and great-great-grands. As people enter into middle and older years, they must adjust to changing physical capacities and increasing losses. The elder generation passes. Sooner or later, most people retire from paid work, engage in various postretirement activities, assume some caregiving for older persons, adapt to their own health concerns and, at very late ages, learn to rely on assistance in daily living.

As people move through developmental stages they are in constant interaction with people at similar and different developmental stages. Expectations about how individuals relate to others in their societies vary from one culture to another, thus norms about human social behavior through the life span vary from one society to another.

Time, the Life Course, and Intergenerational Influences

As individuals grow up, the world around them also changes. Thus the world around a child born in 2005 is quite different from the world around a child born in 1975 or 1945, the generations of their parents and grandparents. A young woman who behaves in a certain way in 2005 carries with her the influences of social forces that were active at the time of her birth 20 years earlier and learned effects of the forces that affected her parent 40 or 50 years earlier. The complex interaction of individual development and life course is a major current field of research (Elder, 1994; Giele & Elder, 1998; Mortimer & Shanahan, 2003) and is guided by the recognition that at any point in the life span, any particular act must be "viewed dynamically as the consequence of past experience and future expectation as well as the integration of individual motive with external constraint" (Giele & Elder, 1998, p. 19).

According to Elder (1994), themes in the life course paradigm include the following: (1) individual lives reflect historical times; (2) social norms create expectations about "social timing," that is, events that take place at expected periods, such as school graduation, settling into a work life, and getting married, and how an individual's life course fits with social timing expectations tells us something about the uniqueness of the individual; (3) human lives are linked, embedded in social relationships with kin and friends who provide social support and regulation; and (4) individuals have human agency, that is, within the constraints of their world, they can plan and make choices that construct their own life courses. The life course paradigm can facilitate the understanding of social relationships within and across generations in a person's social history. Understanding the interdependence of lives can shed light on why a middle-aged woman suffers anxiety for no clear reason except that she was raised by a mother who is a war survivor with posttraumatic stress disorder (PTSD). A child's obesity and eating habits may be affected by his grandparents' habits developed two generations ago, when they had little to eat and so ate their fill whenever they could. Intergenerational conflict in a family may be affected by the markedly different ways each generation sees the world, given its different upbringing in historic context.

Development and the Social History

Conducting a social history assessment requires familiarity with developmental theory about ages and stages, transitional processes, life domains, cultural expectations, and the life course in context. Often people feel encumbered by problems and overlook the normative nature of their life challenges. Even though each human lives a distinct life, all humans share certain common experiences that are explicated by life span developmental science.

Critical Processes in Social Development

How a person becomes a social creature depends on numerous influences. Four factors hold particular prominence in fields of study about human social development. They include theory and knowledge about learning, attachment, stress, and deprivation of nurture.

Learning and Adaptation

Social cognitive theory addresses how behaviors and beliefs are transmitted from one person or group to another. Within the family, children learn actions and attitudes from their parents and other caregivers through social reinforcement, imitation, and modeling. How the child reacts to a parent affects the parents, and so on in a continuing interactional learning process.

According to social cognitive theory, which evolved from social learning theory, behavior is a product of what a person thinks and feels in interaction with the environment (Bandura, 1977, 1997, 2002; Patterson,

1982; Rotter, 1982). How a person behaves in a particular environment is influenced by the person's awareness of factors in the immediate environment and also by acquired beliefs and feelings based on previous life experiences. People develop a relatively consistent set of behaviors that they use across environments, although they are constantly acquiring new perspectives and behaviors, so they are always changing. New factors in the environment or new thoughts can lead to new behaviors.

Social cognitive theory posits that people generally behave in ways that are positively reinforced. In each situation or environment, there are many possible ways the person can behave (potential behaviors) based on what the person knows and can do. The person is likely to choose the behavior associated with highest expectations of positive reinforcement, such as being boisterous if attention is desired, or compliant if praise is needed. Such expectancies are learned through past experiences. Sometimes people have irrational expectancies and can behave in ways that lead to consequences contrary to expectations, as when a gambler irrationally expects that a major win is inevitable and then suffers the agony of repeated losses. The joy of a small win, though, may exceed the agony of defeat in the short term, leading to addictive gambling.

According to Julian Rotter (1982), people develop generalized expectancies, known as locus of control, about whether their behavior will lead to the desired reinforcement. People with a strong internal locus of control believe that they can determine whether or not they achieve the reinforcement. They determine their own success or failure. People with external locus of control often have experienced lack of predictability in their environments, and they have little confidence in their own self-determination. They often attribute outcomes to chance or the power of other people. People may feel more in control in some situations and less control in others.

Albert Bandura (1997) demonstrated that humans learn through social interactions. His studies describe how people pay attention to the behaviors of others, remember the behaviors, and reproduce the behaviors themselves through practice. They are motivated to use the behavior in certain settings depending on the response they get when they try it, judgment about standards that others have for behavior, and expectations they have set for themselves. This is a process of self-regulation. Social order results from groups of people regulating themselves. Disorder occurs when individuals or groups have little capacity for self-regulation.

Bandura's (2002) subsequent research led him to posit that human agency—the capacity to influence one's own life functioning and circumstances—occurs in three typical ways that are culturally influenced.

The ways are individual action; proxy agency, which involves the individual influencing others to act on his or her behalf; and collective agency, which involves collaborating with others. People's abilities to exercise these various forms of agency are affected by their individual capacities and their social and cultural relationships. According to Bandura (2002), the most powerful factor in a person's willingness to exercise any form of agency is perceived efficacy—the belief that the personal, proxy, or collective action will be effective.

Many programs that aim to prevent social problems, such as crime, alcohol or drug abuse, or poor health practices, rely on social cognitive theory. The core elements of the interventions involve teaching and reinforcing positive social behaviors through modeling and contingencies that follow various behaviors. Punishing negative behaviors by creating negative consequences also relies on social learning theory, although extinguishing negative behaviors without replacing them with positive alternatives leads to little change—the person often simply learns other harmful behaviors. The opportunity to experience the positive reinforcement of positive social behavior seems to be an essential developmental process.

Attachment, Emotional Regulation, and Stability in Social Relations

How people feel significantly affects their social functioning. The foundations of emotional development are in attached relationships, learned emotional regulation, and relational stability.

Attachment. Mother Teresa of Calcutta observed, "There is much suffering in the world—very much. And this material suffering is suffering from hunger, suffering from homelessness, from all kinds of diseases, but I still think the greatest suffering is being lonely, feeling unloved, just having no one" (Stern, 2000, p. 7). People learn to love and be loved through their attached relationships. Attachment is a unique relationship that children form with those persons they regard as their sources of security and survival (Ainsworth, 1989; Bowlby, 1969, 1973, 1980). They adore their attachment figures and do whatever they can to be near them. As they grow older and more independent, they seek relationships that are comparable to the one in which they felt attached. People need to feel attached to significant others throughout life.

In the early years, if children's needs for affection, soothing, and human contact go unmet or receive inconsistent responses, they learn to feel frustration and anxiety. Children yearn to be attached. For example, abused and neglected children are remarkably loyal to their abusers (Carnes, 1997). They continuously seek their love and approval. They do what they can to help and protect their abusive parents. Even when children are alienated from their parents and say they hate them, children tend to feel esteem for their parents and regret that they cannot feel positive about them. They don't want to think of their parents as bad, so they regard themselves as bad. The parent acts as if the child were bad, and because the parent is powerful, that reinforces the child's distorted thinking. Self-esteem plummets, and these children blame themselves for their plight.

Early attachments as well as the experience of various attached relationships throughout development affect how adults form later attachments (Collins, Guichard, & Ford, 2004). Life experiences lead some adults to have serial relationships with limited attachments while others are able to bond for life.

Emotional and Behavioral Regulation. From infancy onward, humans learn to regulate their emotions. Eisenberg, Fabes, Guthrie, and Reiser (2001) define emotion regulation as "the process of initiating, maintaining, modulating, or changing the occurrence, intensity, or duration of internal feeling states and emotion-related physiological processes, often in the service of accomplishing one's goals" (p. 48). Regulation occurs through managing attention (e.g., shifting attention and focus or using cognitive distraction), cognitive reinterpretation of the situation, and neurophysiological processes. Much regulation occurs after the emotions emerge, but people can anticipate emotions and adjust their environments or situations to reduce the likelihood that an emotion will emerge.

People also learn to regulate the behavioral expressions of emotion (Gross, 1998). They can learn to control their facial expressions and activate or restrain certain behaviors (e.g., crying, moving the body). Much of emotional regulation and behavioral expression is not conscious or by rational or voluntary intent of the person. It often happens involuntarily. People tend to become engaged in patterns of emotional regulation that fall into three groups: (1) optimally regulated, (2) highly inhibited, and (3) undercontrolled. Optimally regulated individuals may have high levels of negative emotions but they are socially competent and behaviorally constructive. Highly inhibited individuals are rigid, constrained, and prone to regulations by others. Undercontrolled individuals tend to be impulsive and poor problem solvers.

People regulate their emotions within the context of their social interactions. Children, for example, who are undercontrolled but have a preponderance of positive emotions and high degrees of resilience may have positive social adjustment. On the other hand, those who are undercontrolled and have multiple negative emotions and low resilience may develop serious social problems.

The growth of self-regulation in social behavior is a cornerstone of early child development that cuts across all domains of behavior (Shonkoff & Phillips, 2000). Self-regulation is physiological (i.e., the body regulates its own temperature and digests food to convert it to energy) and behavioral (e.g., toilet training, learning to wait for food, or learning to avoid danger). In U.S. culture, examples of typically regulated behavior at various ages are the following: sit still and listen (age 6), do coordinated games (age 8), pass complex tests (age 10), control sexual urges (age 12), show respect for authority (age 14), and contribute to one's own income (age 18). Regulation is acquired through good nurture and the process of social learning.

Connecting with others in genuine communication requires empathic understanding of what the other person is feeling. People learn the capacity for empathy through securely attached relationships in which parents regulate their emotions and reinforce children to regulate theirs, too. Empathy is the root of social responsibility, conscience, and positive moral behavior (Thompson, 1998).

Stability. To be effective, nurturing behavior by caregivers must occur on a fairly regular basis over extended periods of time (Bronfenbrenner, 1999). Childhood "turbulence" clearly interferes with healthy development. Children are at risk of problematic developmental outcomes if they experience environmental instability (e.g., frequent residential moves or changing household members, changing child care or schools), lack of clear structure (e.g., irregular daily routines or inconsistency in parental expectations), injuries or illness, and unpredictability of events (e.g., parental temper outbursts or unexplained parental absences; Hetherington & Clingempeel, 1992).

Low-income families are more likely than nonpoor families to experience changes in household or family composition, arrest or incarceration of parents, family violence, involvement in the child welfare system (including periods of foster care), and unstable child care, leading to disrupted attachments for the child (Brooks-Gunn, Duncan, & Aber, 1997). The more change, the more risk to the child (Moore, Vandivere, & Ehrle,

2000). Frequent moves in residence among poor families significantly reduce their accumulation of social capital (Duncan, 1996; Hagan, MacMillan, & Wheaton, 1996; Tucker, Marx, & Long, 1998) and their academic performance (Eckenrode, Rowe, Laird, & Brathwaite, 1995).

People who have an unpredictable and anxious sense of self in relation to others are often yearning for acceptance and approval (Ainsworth, 1989). They have difficulty separating their feelings from their thoughts and often act based on how they feel, rather than thinking through the logical consequences of their behavior. This tendency can induce a cycle of negative social interactions that leads to more rather than less anxiety. Consistent affirmation from unchanging caregivers can prevent or alleviate such social anxiety.

During the early years of development, a degree of order and predictability in the child's social world promotes attachment and emotional and behavioral regulation. Excessive transitions and social instability create demands, even chaos, that interfere with the child's mastery of social situations. Stability facilitates the child's acquisition of social skills that allow him or her to adaptively give and receive within social relationships.

Stress, Coping, Vulnerability, and Resilience

Life tends to be relatively predictable until something happens, suddenly or gradually, that disrupts the sense of balance. Environmental factors that lead to stress are known as stressors. Stress, a physiological and psychological state, is a signal that people need to adapt because they are exceeding their capacity to manage a situation (Lazarus, 2000). Coping behaviors are a learned repertoire of actions that can reduce stress. Examples of adaptive coping that can lead to stress reduction are releasing pent-up energy through exercise, relieving fatigue through rest, or releasing sadness through crying. Coping can also be maladaptive, as when people drink alcohol repeatedly or to the point of intoxication, which relieves stress for the short term, but can increase stress for the longer term. Using physical force to quiet a loud child can accomplish short-term relief from the noise, but leads to side effects that create more stress later, such as the child's learned use of force.

Stressors include those that are expected and normative, such as changing jobs, death of an elderly parent, city traffic, or a young adult child leaving home. They may also be unexpected, as when a young child dies or a storm damages one's residence. If they include a serious threat to life or involve a major loss, they are regarded as catastrophic or traumatic.

No stressor can be regarded as a discrete event, although it can be recorded and measured as such. Each event is preceded by antecedent events and triggers a series of subsequent events. For example, a particularly severe child beating is preceded by a series of long-term and immediate events that culminate in the parent's aggression and the child's forced participation. The beating is followed by various events that may promote healing or induce physical or psychological damage. Another example is that divorce is often regarded as an event that ends a relationship when in fact it is a never-ending story if children are involved; the relationship between the parents does not end, it just assumes a new form and dynamics.

Cumulative stress that results from multiple stressors and losses can erode an individual's or family's capacity to manage stress, leading to maladaptive coping (Catherill, 2004). Persistent stress induces behavioral problems such as lower frustration tolerance, irritability, and negative social interactions (Evans, 1999). Some families confront a stunning mul-tiplicity of stressors, such as domestic violence, homelessness, income inse-curity, disability, and discrimination, all at once (Kagan & Schlosberg, 1989). Once a person's stress management system starts to fail, vulnera-bility to additional crises increases. Sometimes, multiple crises emerge from poor judgment related to a stressed condition or real helplessness due to limited options created by multiple stressors. Other times, people just face substantial misfortune.

Resilient individuals are able to confront life's challenges and emerge stronger than they were before the crisis. They are neither merely survivors nor are they rugged individuals oblivious to the pain. Rather, they have absorbed the experience in ways that allow them to learn from it and use their lessons to handle future problems. Resilience helps to explain why some children survive childhood abuse without mental illness or propen-sity for being abusive or are able to rise above their origins in poverty (Dugan & Coles, 1989; Garbarino, 1997; Garmezy, 1991; Simeonsson, 1995). Resilient families use interactional processes to rebound from dis-ruptive life challenges (McCubbin, McCubbin, McCubbin, & Futrell, 1995; McCubbin, McCubbin, Thompson, & Fromer, 1995; Walsh, 1998). "Hardiness" is a similar concept and refers to individuals or fami-lies that are able to withstand stress without becoming ill (Kobasa, 1985).

By contrast, vulnerable individuals succumb in various ways to the forces of acute or chronic stress; their responses are maladaptive. They may develop physical illnesses, particularly heart disease and immune sys-tem deficiencies. They may develop a range of mental illnesses, including those specifically linked to stress, such as posttraumatic stress disorder or mood disorders such as depression or anxiety. In extreme cases, their minds seek to block the perceptions that induce stress and they dissociate or develop other psychotic or perceptual distortions. Grasping for relief from the stress, they may externalize their distress and develop oppositional patterns of behaving, such as using physical force or engaging in manipulative or subversive activities that are illegal.

Resilience seems to evolve from biological and social sources (Dugan & Coles, 1989). The individual capacity to manage physical stress is regulated by biochemical functions that genetically vary from one individual to another and are apparent soon after birth. In addition, the individual can acquire certain conditions that inhibit the biological capacity for stress management, as in the case of certain head injuries, brain tumors, depletion by constant exposure to highly demanding stressors, alteration subsequent to use of chemicals or medications, or some physical diseases that compromise the endocrine system.

Resilience can be fostered by social learning, which is the goal of many current mental health prevention interventions. Resilient people tend to have high levels of perceived personal control (i.e., they believe they are not helpless and are confident they can influence the world around them) and self-esteem (i.e., they like themselves and their lives and believe others like them, too). This "learned optimism" derives essentially from beliefs that are grounded in a worldview that has been influenced by family belief systems and personal experience, including spiritual and moral lessons (Seligman, 1995). Froma Walsh (1998, p. 24) summarizes the characteristics of resilient families according to three factors:

1. Family belief systems help them make meaning of adversity, hold positive outlooks, and transcend their experience, perhaps through spirituality.

2. Family organizational patterns allow flexibility, connectedness, and flow of social and economic resources to help with the challenge.

3. Family communication processes are clear, emotionally open, and based on collaborative problem solving.

The vulnerable person's beliefs tend to be pessimistic. People who see themselves as vulnerable believe they are helpless and may even demonstrate "surplus powerlessness," which is the belief that one is less powerful than objective observers would believe one to be (Lerner, 1991). This occurs particularly in individuals who are relatively free after long periods of extreme oppression. Adult survivors of chronic physical or sexual abuse and survivors of human trafficking or genocidal campaigns are at greatest risk for surplus powerlessness (Mack, 1994).

The impact of stress seems to be mediated by several factors associated with the persons, the nature of the stressor, and the coping environment. For example, various studies (Briere & Elliott, 1994; Hopper, 2006; Tremblay, Herbert, & Piche, 1999) suggest that abused children are most at risk of long-term effects if the following factors are present:

- Abuse occurs when the child is young.
- Abuse is committed by an attached caregiver or trusted person.
- When the harm becomes known, people respond in unhelpful ways.
- The violence is severe.
- The abuse continued for a long time.
- Multiple offenders harm the child.
- The abuse involved humiliating the child.
- The abuse is not "normal" within the family or culture or the child is singled out for maltreatment.
- The child has no relationships in which negative feelings can be constructively expressed.
- The child believes no one or few people love him or her.
- The child has no consistent positive relationships in his or her social network outside the family.

Conversely, children abused under conditions that do not meet the above criteria may be at lower risk of long-term psychological or social problems.

People cannot avoid coping. They do something to address their stress. For example, a girl may be in persistent danger due to domestic violence and frequent street violence in her neighborhood. She learns not to rely on adults for protection; the adults are often unable to protect themselves. She develops no trust in formal protective services such as law enforcement, child welfare services, or school officials, because their efforts to help are usually brief and ineffectual and may even cause more trouble than good. Each of them has the capacity to harm others even if they are trying to help. She finds ways to protect herself by hiding under beds and in closets, using "get-away paths" in the neighborhood, forming coalitions with family members, and joining a gang outside the home. She seeks ways to change her internal state of anxiety by getting numb through alcohol or drugs, plugging in earphones for loud music, and staying glued to the TV. She learns to minimize or deny the impact of any abuse she repeatedly suffers. She may dissociate, split off memories of experiences so they do not intrude and evoke feelings of fear and anxiety. She does what she can to reduce perceived stress. The withdrawn existence of this damaged and deprived child does not doom her for life. She can unlearn her ways of coping and learn newer, healthier ways, but the more entrenched her habits become, the harder they will be to break.

Resilient children possess a set of protective factors that buffer them against stress and contribute to positive individualized responses to risk. Protective factors fall into three categories: (1) dispositional factors of the child, (2) familial factors, and (3) external support systems (Garmezy, 1985; Kirby & Fraser, 1997). Michael Rutter (1987) asserts that protective mechanisms interact with risk variables and block the potential effect of stress. He suggests four mechanisms that may act as predictors in the protective process: (1) reduction of risk impact, (2) reduction of negative chain reactions, (3) establishment and maintenance of self-esteem and self-efficacy, and (4) opening up of opportunities. A child's resilience is fostered if someone or a group of people acts assertively to mobilize these mechanisms. That is, they are proactively protecting the child's physical and emotional well-being.

How children cope depends significantly on how their family system copes. Froma Walsh's (1998) summary of findings from research regarding family resilience identifies these factors as critical to positive coping and resilience: (1) belief systems that make meaning of adversity, positive outlook, and transcendence and spirituality; (2) organizational patterns within the family that allow for flexibility, connectedness, and flow of social resources; and (3) communication processes that are clear, open, and collaborative. When confronted with stressors, family members of all ages benefit if their family systems have these resilience-promoting characteristics.

Effects of Trauma or Loss and Unresolved Grief. Certain stressors, particularly those that are traumatic or involve a major loss, require major life adaptations (Janoff-Bulman, 1992). The person must grieve the loss of old ways of being and learn to embrace new ways.

Traumatic stressors expose persons to actual or threatened death or injury to themselves or others. When confronting a traumatic stressor, most people feel overwhelming fear, helplessness, or horror (Van der Kolk, McFarlane, & Weisaeth, 1996). They experience traumatic stress for a short time after the event, including feeling that they are going crazy or developing a mental illness. They may have uncontrollable emotions fluctuating with numbness, as if they cannot feel anything. They are likely to have sleep and eating disturbances or other physical ailments. They find they have flashbacks to images of the event and have difficulty concentrating on routine tasks of daily living. They work hard to avoid anything that reminds them of the event or become obsessed with reliving it. Such symptoms for a month or few weeks are typical; they are normal, acute responses to an abnormal event. Symptoms that do not subside or that persist for 6 months or more may indicate the person has posttraumatic stress disorder.

Coping with traumatic stress will take exceptional resources. Often, people need extra social support, new information, and more time than when facing other serious stressors. When long-term posttraumatic effects occur, the process requires extended recovery to attain a sense of normalcy again. In general, people are never quite the same, but they can gain a fresh sense of mastery and even feel they have gained certain strengths or attributes as they go through recovery. People with inadequate coping and recovery may develop serious or chronic psychiatric or behavior problems.

Whether the major stressor is traumatic or related to another loss, such as a change in lifestyle and residence that occurs due to a community's economic failure, the person must grieve for what has been lost. Walsh (1998) observes, "By and large, the mental health field has failed to appreciate the impact of loss on the family as an interactional system" (p. 175). The harmful physical and mental health effects of unresolved grief are well documented (Walsh & McGoldrick, 1991). Loss precipitates grief and a period of mourning that, if poorly resolved, can lead to negative development or even serious pathology.

People face many potential losses. They experience disrupted relationships through death of loved ones, relocation, divorce, or termination of a long-term relationship. They may need to adapt to a disability acquired through accident or illness. They must adjust to extended absences of family members due to military service, incarceration, or desertion. They face disappointment such as failure in sports, academics, or talent. They may lose their hopes and dreams. Some must cope with what Bruce and Schultz (2001) call "nonfinite grief," the continual and recurring confrontation with perceived loss due to disparities between expectations and reality, as when they are managing a declining health condition or supporting a family member with a disability.

Death of loved ones precipitates significant grief. When the death is unexpected, violent, or the result of suicide, the risk of damage is particularly high. While the mourning process helps individuals to adapt, from a child's perspective, loss of a significant loved one changes the child's entire support network, and letting go of the yearning for contact with the lost one is only part of the challenge—learning to adapt to life without the support is a major new developmental task (Webb, 2002). How children adapt depends on their cognitive and developmental capacity, the type of support they receive from surviving adults, and the amount of support they have lost. In general, U.S. culture provides few supports to help children cope with loss; talk of death is avoided; even religious beliefs promote the idea that death is unreal and only temporary. Rituals are quick and final and people are encouraged to move quickly through mourning, to "adjust." In some families the aftermath of death precipitates intense conflicts. In others, recovery from grief leads to new opportunities.

The recovery process starts as soon as the loss is realized or the traumatic event is over. A person's long-term development can be significantly enhanced if the recovery environment is supportive, allowing for free expression of emotional concerns, making restitution for losses to the extent possible, and providing information or materials essential to regaining a sense of wholeness.

Deprivation

While loss involves being deprived of something valuable that was formerly present, primary deprivation involves the absence of something that never was. Deprivation during development may be the most profound negative influence on a human. Trauma presumes a preexisting condition of relative normalcy that is disrupted by an extraordinary impact. With profound primary deprivation, something that should have happened to promote healthy development never did, so there is no preexisting normalcy. Primary deprivation, termed deprivation in the following discussion, is distinguished from loss, which can be regarded as form of deprivation that involves absence of something valuable that was present for a while.

Deprivation occurs among children who are rich and poor, black, brown, or white, girls or boys, from all walks of life, but it is most common among children who are economically poor. Knowledge in the mental health field has advanced substantially regarding how humans react to threats (trauma). Far less attention has focused on what happens when a child is deprived of nurture or stimulation, except in cases of extreme deprivation. Deprivation can be divided into three categories: absolute, relative, and perceived.

Absolute Deprivation. Certain developmental needs are absolute: food, water, protection, and nurturing touch. Without them, infants and children die. The key question is: How much is enough?

Research has found that infants who are not touched will basically become suicidal and refuse food, developing a syndrome known as "nonorganic failure to thrive" (Sirotnak, 2003). Anna Freud (Freud & Burlingham, 1944) watched children die in large orphanages after World War II and recognized this syndrome. Instituting a regular practice of nurses' cuddling the babies virtually eliminated the death rate. But if a little bit of touch is essential for survival, how much is enough for healthy development, for forming emotional bonds? These emotional bonds create patterns in the brain that make human interaction pleasant and form the basis for later development of empathy, the capacity to understand what another is feeling. Knowing whether a baby was cuddled and knowing something about the emotional state of the cuddler gives us a clue about whether deprivation may have occurred. Young children who lack at least one loving and consistent adult often suffer severe and long-lasting developmental difficulties, including detachment disorder, which inhibits their ability to form lasting social relationships (Shonkoff & Phillips, 2000).

Relative Deprivation. While some developmental needs are absolute, others are relative, determined by the culture and subculture in which a child resides. Developmental expectations change over time. For example, in the United States in 2005, children are expected to enter first grade at about age 6 ready to learn to read, write, and do math. States monitor "school readiness" indicators to see how children as a population enter schools ("Rhode Island Kids Count," 2005). Also in U.S. culture, at some point each year, children can expect special attention from adults celebrating their childish status: on their birthday, at Hanukkah, or Christmas, perhaps. By law, parents are responsible for their children, as compared to other cultures where the extended family or state have clearly delegated responsibilities for promoting a child's development. When children are denied typical opportunities that are essential for healthy development within their cultures, such as those who have no early childhood stimuli to help them get ready for school, or never have anyone recognize special days for them, or have no parents to care for them, they are considered deprived according to social norms.

Childhood living conditions vary dramatically across and within communities (Corcoran, 1995; Duncan & Brooks-Gunn, 1997; McLoyd,

1998). Resources and opportunities have never been equitably distributed among children. Disparities between those who "have" and those who "have not" can be vast. A child's fortune is substantially determined by circumstances of birth: national origin; familial social, racial, or ethnic identity and socioeconomic class; geographic location; gender; physical and mental ability; or other factors. Across the world, classes of children are excluded, marginalized, and exploited. Circumstances often change during a child's development, but many children confront persistent deprivation while others are indulged by privilege. This relative deprivation can have a profound impact on a child's development by creating disadvantages and barriers to opportunities that other children have.

Significant caregiver mental health problems, such as maternal depression, substance abuse, or family violence, impose heavy developmental burdens. Most often, the process whereby these conditions affect the child involve deprivation of some kind. For example, a mother can be so depressed she cannot attend to the child. The battered mother can be so preoccupied with trying to prevent the battering that she ignores the child. The mentally ill parent may be absent for periods of hospitalization. An increasingly common situation is for a child to be abandoned by one parent, most often the father. Children can be relatively deprived for many reasons that are culturally determined by their communities and societies.

Perceived Deprivation. Children can also *feel* relatively deprived because of frustrated desires, not just unmet needs. A classic example is sibling rivalry. Some parents do in fact favor one child over another; even outside observers see the obvious favoritism. The less favored child is relatively deprived of parental attention. Yet some children *feel* relatively unwanted, no matter how hard the parent tries to treat them equally and fairly. Such a child feels deprived.

The term *affluenza* was coined to refer to a developed world (particularly U.S.) phenomenon that involves insatiable craving for material goods (deGraaf, Wann, & Naylor, 2001). People with this affliction constantly feel deprived, even though they are surrounded by material and, sometimes, emotional plenty. This is different from emotional disturbance and feelings of yearning among people with plenty who had earlier periods of actual neglect. For example, children adopted after childhood neglect into well-supplied homes often hoard food or show signs of mistrust, which are indicators of perceived deprivation. Children with affluenza believe themselves to be deprived of material goods and suffer resentment even though they have always had plenty. While perceived deprivation may not pose the threats to life and well-being that absolute deprivation does, it can lead to mental health problems, even suicide or aggression toward others.

Assessing any level of deprivation is significant in understanding a social history. Deprivation comes from relationships with others as resources that should be transferred from one person to another are not, or are perceived to be withheld. Understanding actual or perceived deprivation can provide insight into a person's social functioning.

Summary

As a foundation for social history assessment, theories that explain human social development offer a language for organizing patterns and themes as the life story unfolds. Social behavior emerges from a complex interplay among individual and environmental factors. The lifelong process of individual social, physical, mental, spiritual, and moral development involves constant learning and adaptation as the environment influences the individual and vice versa. As people with their unique innate and acquired traits pass through life experiences, how they adapt influences their subsequent well-being positively and negatively. Normative standards and expectations about social roles vary by culture and setting, which helps to explain why people act differently according to traits such as age, ethnicity, or gender and in different relationships, such as with partners, family, coworkers, or friends.

Social functioning is particularly affected by the person's history of attachment, emotional regulation, stability in social relations, and unique experiences, particularly those that induce various levels of stress and elicit various ways of coping by the individual. In addition, people often are quite conscious of when something happened to them, but may be less aware of how they were deprived—they don't know what they missed. A professional who understands normative social development within a cultural context and coping processes will have a clear lens through which to interpret a social history in a way that sheds light on how the various people and experiences in the history affected the individual's social development.

3

The Professional Lens, Part II

Social Ecology of Human Development and Behavior

Individuals are born and live embedded in social environments made up of caregiving and threatening forces nested in the family, social network, neighborhood, broader community, and society (Bronfenbrenner, 2005a, 2005b; Germain, 1991). A person's social history evolves in this ecological context. A review of basic social systems theory will lay a foundation for subsequent discussion of how various ecological factors influence social development and behavior.

Environmental Context and Social Systems Theory

The constellation of social factors that surround an individual can be conceptualized as a social system (see Figure 3.1). Intricately complex, social systems can be described using concepts from general systems theory, which originated in biology in 1936 (Bertalanffy, 1968). Systems essentially are dynamic entities that maintain some degree of order and boundaries while perpetually changing. Elements within the system exchange resources, such as energy and information, among themselves and with the external environment. "Static" systems are resistant to change and do so slowly. "Dynamic" systems change rapidly. "Closed" systems have tight boundaries and exchange only internally, not with the external environment.

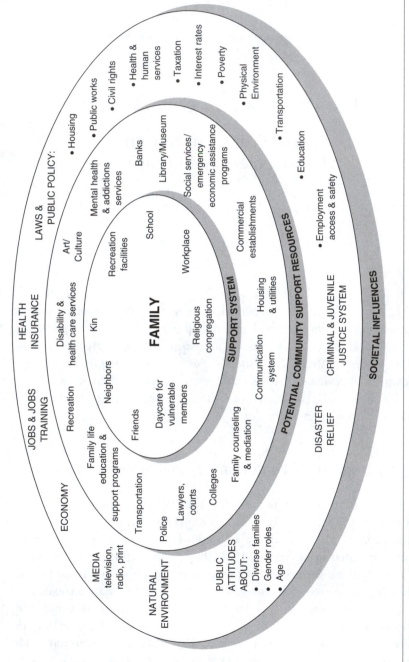

Figure 3.1 The Family in Community: An Ecological Perspective

"Open" systems exchange freely or through self-regulation with the external environment. Systems that develop rigid order and energy over time are "entropic" and those that lose energy and dissolve into chaos are "negentropic." To survive, a system must aim for a stable balance between internal control and regulation of relations with the broader environment; the system does this through adaptation. Systems have characteristics that are greater than and different from the sum of their parts. Every part of a system affects every other part of the system; they are interdependent. Within a system, some elements are organized into subsystems. Outside the system, environments are composed of multiple, overlapping systems.

Social systems can be understood in terms of their structures and their processes (Luhmann, 1995). Describing a social system involves identifying the parts, attributing qualities to the parts and the whole system, describing how the relationships work among the parts and with the broader environment, and describing key characteristics of the broader environment.

Structurally, the parts are people, including individuals and subsystems of people as small as a couple to as large as a community or organization. Systems and their parts may possess a vast array of qualities, illustrated by such terms as *cohesive, unstable, well differentiated, enmeshed, flexible, chaotic, fragmented,* or *weakly bonded.* Systems theory provides a framework for describing, understanding, and acting to change the dynamic processes and structure of human relationships. The language of systems theory permeates most helping professions.

The system that exerts the most substantial influence on an individual's social history is the family, which can be defined as "an organized, interdependent system, regulated by a set of norms and rules" (Gerson, 1995, p. 91). Members of a family include those who share a household and others who live beyond it. McGoldrick, Gerson, and Shellenberger (1999) offer an encompassing definition: "Family is, by our definition, those who are tied together through their common biological, legal, cultural, and emotional history and their implied future together" (p. 7). The norms and rules guide interactions among the family members; thus the relationships tend to follow particular patterns. As the family evolves through time and its members go through life transitions and respond to interactions with the external environment, the rules change. How the family handles these transitions affects the well-being of its members.

Similarly, the influence of other social systems, such as the school, peer network, or faith community, on individual or group development can be described through systems theory. How these factors typically influence human development and behavior will be addressed in more detail after another core concept, development, is discussed.

Family and Social Networks as Mediators of Individual Behavior

Humans' earliest and most consistent social contexts are their families, which change throughout their life course. What is learned in the family is transferred to other social contexts. Likewise, as the child develops and spends more time away from the family, what is learned in external contexts affects the family. Various family members bring to the family beliefs and behaviors they have learned in other contexts. This constant interaction of the family with external social environments places demands on the family that require family members to adapt. Given that each family member is also progressing through her or his own development, collectively the family has its own unique developmental life cycle.

Families can be understood in terms of their structures, processes, and resources. Variations in individual behavior are affected by differences in these family capacities. In addition, an individual's behavior may be influenced by the genetic inheritance from within the biological family.

Family Structure

Discussions of family conditions often center on family structure, which has always changed according to adaptations necessary for particular cultural and historical contexts. Structurally, families may include grandparents (increasingly, more than one generation of grands as people live 80 or 90 years or more), mother, father, children, step-relatives, half-siblings, aunts, uncles, cousins, and people related by blood or marriage (current or former). Some families, like foster and adoptive families or gay or lesbian-headed households, are connected by chosen commitments. Sometimes family members live together, sometimes in separate households. A particular family's composition changes periodically, but its basic functions are constant, as noted here:

> Far from being static, families are dynamic units engaged in an intertwined process of individual and group development. They can be viewed from three different perspectives. First, a family can be seen as a biological unit whose members are linked together by blood ties; this

relationship is often institutionalized through marriage or sanctioned by an equivalent relationship and describes the kinship between mothers, fathers, and their children. Secondly, a family can be seen as a social unit consisting of a number of people, who usually live together in the same household and share different developmental tasks and social functions. Thirdly, a family can be seen as a psychological unit defined around the personal feelings and emotional bonds of its members. (United Nations, 1994, p. 1)

Families come in all shapes and sizes, but they are influenced by the social norms inherent in their immediate culture and the larger society around them. Some of the norms pertain to the authority or leadership structure of the family. For example, in "traditional" families with rigid gender roles, men relate to the outside world and women to the home. Females are subordinate to males, and men are only marginally involved in rearing young children. In authoritarian families, the patriarch takes control if women or children defy their expected roles and "step out of line." Historically, this involved the sanctioned use of physical force, even death, to maintain order. In such societies, father absence does not mean that men are not regarded as authority figures in the family. Men who pass through a household or assume fathering roles are often accorded deference under the traditional model. Even where females assume most economic as well as social responsibilities for the family, male privilege may still prevail.

Alternatively, an egalitarian family strives for consensus among members or cooperatively delegates authority over certain matters to various members. For example, a mechanically inclined member may have control over the garage, while the one with culinary skills rules the kitchen. The less predictable circumstances in an egalitarian family require clear and open communication to prevent confusion or conflict. These families engage in routine collaborative problem solving, or carry unresolved tension.

How families organize their structure varies widely. As each family is formed, it blends the practices of the members' families of origin; as people develop, or circumstances change, the family structure and organization also evolve. For example, when a spouse dies, someone assumes that person's roles. When a parent leaves a household due to divorce, the other parent must adapt.

Within the family system, a healthy family has clear boundaries between its members and respect for the integrity of each person (Bowen, 1985; Minuchin, Colapinto, & Minuchin, 1998). Each person understands his or her role in the family. This is known as differentiation; in a well differentiated family, there is high tolerance for difference and members respect one another. Children whose boundaries are violated, for example, when adults in the household abuse them sexually, often develop no clear sense of how they are distinct from others. As adults, they may easily disclose private matters to strangers and fail to see the social norms that govern privacy and integrity of individuals. Families with rigid internal boundaries, such as strict patriarchies where the father makes all decisions, can produce children who are poorly prepared to handle flexibility or to make autonomous decisions when such are expected. Thus, if a dominant peer tells them to perform an illegal act, they may feel confused about what to do and comply because it is all they know how to do. Healthy young adults differentiate themselves from their families of origin, resolve negative emotions about letting go, and maintain open and respectful relationships with their families of origin.

The family also has boundaries with regard to the external environment, including identification of who is in the family and who is not. Open families welcome people to come in as family members and are tolerant when they leave. For example, a child may have several unrelated people to call "uncle" or "stepmother" as the child's primary parent engages in serial live-in relationships. In such cases, if the needs of the child are overlooked, the child may develop no clear sense of who is in the family and how to identify him- or herself. Other families may be disengaged, with rigid boundaries for each person and limited communication among them so that each family member has an autonomous life while sharing a household or identity. At a different extreme, tightly closed families cut themselves off from the world and deprive members of normal interactions with others, thus equipping children poorly to deal with experiences outside the home if and when they do become independent. Families may be enmeshed, with strong pressure for togetherness, diffuse boundaries among individuals, and no room for privacy or independence. The variations in family functioning are infinite.

Individuals learn from their family systems and carry ways of relating into other social relationships. For example, Murray Bowen (1985) observes that adults with poor differentiation of self tend to engage in relationships outside the family that are marked by (1) conflict and high emotional reactivity (to maintain distance from others), (2) dominance (i.e., they seek to relate to people they can control) or child-like dependence (i.e., they find a parental figure who will provide the care and support they crave), and (3) projection of anxiety onto their own children (i.e., they may overindulge or treat their children harshly based on projected beliefs that the child is fragile or is oppositional). Generally, each of these relational patterns leads to personal dysfunction and harm to others in the relationship. People from dysfunctional families have uncanny ways of finding partners to perpetuate these patterns.

Healthy families have a clear sense of who is in and who is not, and have open communication with outsiders. They balance the unity of the family with the separateness of each individual. Each person has individual identity with commitment to the family group.

Family members may form coalitions within the nuclear or the extended family system. Some are beneficial to family well-being, as when parents are together in their approach to childrearing. Others can breed harm, such as when a parent coalesces with a favored child and grants that child privileges while the rest of the family is excluded. Coalitions within the family system may develop conflicts among members.

Using a life course perspective, social norms about family structure can be seen to change over time within any particular society. For example, in the United States at the beginning of the 21st century, while family structures are extraordinarily diverse, the general trends are that young adults cohabit before marriage, birth to unmarried mothers is increasing, mothers with children (whether married, cohabiting, or without a partner) work outside the home, nearly half of all children will live with a single parent for part of their lives, the majority of adults will marry more than once, acceptance of same-sex marriage is increasing, and 42% of people over age 65 will require long-term care in their own homes or alternate placements (LTC Info, 2003). These patterns differ significantly from patterns at the turn of the 20th century, when "traditional" families—those with a biological father and mother—were the norm.

Family Processes

How a family manages life's gifts and threats depends on the dynamics of the family system. The exchange of information, ideas, and feelings within a family is governed by rules and expectations that are unique to each family.

Froma Walsh (1998) emphasizes that a family's fundamental beliefs about itself guide the ways members interact with one another and the outside world. She identifies several core beliefs that characterize families that manage to be resilient in the face of adversity. These include *trust*—faith in the dependability of and loyalty to one another; *coherence*—the belief that life has meaning and is manageable despite continual shifts; *respect* for individual differences and autonomy; a sense of *shared history and identity*;

positive outlook—commitment to persevere and to hope for the future; *acceptance* of things that cannot be changed; belief in *transcendence*, a greater whole beyond oneself; and *spirituality* that is dynamic and provides support.

Family processes essentially involve communication: Who communicates with whom about what, with what tone? Communication takes many forms, including those that are verbal and nonverbal, and those that are spoken, written, sung, illustrated, enacted, or otherwise transmitted. Functional families have clear communication; the sender of a message is clear, and the receiver can send feedback that the message is clearly received. Messages include rational thoughts as well as a wide range of emotions. Family members know how to share joy, sorrow, affection, anger, and a host of other feelings. Expression of negativity is tolerated. These families solve problems by collaboratively identifying the problem, exploring alternative solutions, sharing decisions about what to do, evaluating the effect of decisions, and trying again if necessary. They negotiate, compromise, reciprocate, and constructively manage conflict. They adapt constructively.

By contrast, families may have a variety of dysfunctional communication patterns. For example, children who engage in crime tend to come from homes with high turmoil, inconsistent consequences for behavior, and excessive coercion by parents (Reid, Patterson, & Snyder, 2002). These children learn to try to coerce others to get their way, the parents respond with increasing coercion, and the cycle escalates as the child becomes increasingly resistant. The family adapts in destructive ways, and stress mounts. Without help from outside resources, the family is at risk of serious problems.

What works to promote harmony in one family may not work in another. By tradition, some families are more comfortable with hierarchical decision making. Others prefer egalitarian communication. As families form, the members bring their experiences and habits from their families of origin. Together, they form a new family system with its own processes and communications norms. The extent to which these processes promote healthy and socially adaptable behavior in each family member will vary from one family to another and over time within a family.

Family Resources

To survive, families must exchange resources with the external environment. They gather resources to meet physical needs, such as food, shelter, clothing, hygiene, health care, and transportation. Healthy families distribute these resources among their members along with emotional support and a sense of belonging over time. They take particular care of vulnerable family members, that is, those who are young, very old, or have special needs.

The key medium for resource exchange is work. During the early years, a person's work is typically in educational settings; later it is in paid or voluntary employment in exchange for money, goods, or status. School and work environments exert significant influences on family systems, and vice versa. A person's various occupations and the quality of the work environments can promote or hinder life satisfaction.

Families also exchange resources through their social networks. Social *network* refers to the structure of a person's social system, that is, the number and type of people with whom the person interacts. Social *support* pertains to functions of the system, including emotional and instrumental positive interactions such as providing a listening ear or a shoulder to cry on or giving concrete aid such as food or transportation (Haines, Beggs, & Hurlbert, 2002). The person may regard the social interaction positively, negatively, ambivalently (both positively and negatively), or benignly. Generally, positive networks of adequate size help families cope with life's demands (Coyne & Downey, 1991). Some people have large networks, but if their networks provide little positive support, these people may still struggle as if they were alone.

Families with adequate internal resources manage, with relative ease, to garner not only what they need but also what they desire from their communities. Their lives are not without problems, but they generally can overcome access barriers and benefit from high quality health care and education, fair access to justice, and other such privileges. Families who have been historically denied adequate resources or have become marginalized fare less well. They suffer the burden of disparities. Many feel politically impotent, economically oppressed, and psychologically helpless in community arenas outside the comforting circle of their own family and friends. They struggle with unemployment or poor job conditions, racial and ethnic discrimination, inferior schools, deprived child and elder care, and insufficient health and mental health care. Even when marginal groups gather strength, their more endowed neighbors tend to gather even greater strength, and the relative disparities persist. This dynamic makes for fragile and fragmented communities rather than strong, sustainable communities.

Behavioral Genetics

People inherit their genes from their biological ancestors. The ways in which people interact within their environments, including how they relate to those with whom they share a gene pool, are complex. The next decade will bring forth major discoveries with regard to specific genetic influences on behavior, thanks to the rapid advances in the field of genetic research. On April 14, 2003, the International Human Genome Sequencing Consortium announced it had completed the sequence of the human genome (Collins, Green, Guttmacher, & Guyer, 2003). The discovery confirmed that all humans share most of their genetic composition (99.9%) and that individuals vary considerably within their unique 0.01% genetic constitution. Some of this genetic variation is shared with their biological families of origin. Research has enabled the identification of genes associated with diseases such as diabetes and schizophrenia and certain behavioral and physical traits, though the initial studies have emphasized the complexity of the etiology of various conditions and the need for much more substantial research (Bonham, Warshauer-Baker, & Collins, 2005).

Scientists agree that genetic factors are some of the many factors that help to explain human behavior but they never are the exclusive explanation (Plomin & Daniels, 1987). For example, research has demonstrated that the propensity for aggression in childhood may be heritable but its manifestation depends on environmental influences (DiLalla, 2002; Plomin, DeFries, & McClearn, 1990). Behavior patterns tend to run in families, but the extent to which they are genetically determined (i.e., based in biological functions determined by genes) or environmentally determined (i.e., based in social learning) varies from one situation to another. Genetic and environmental factors are correlated and interactive. Genetics do not determine behavior, but they can make it possible, so that under certain environmental conditions, the behavior occurs.

Thus far, research has found a genetic predisposition for behavior associated with such capacities as: cognitive reasoning (though no genetic link has been shown for memory or cognitive creativity); achievement in particular academic areas; reading disability; mental retardation; certain dementias; schizophrenia; depression; anxiety disorders; alcoholism; extraversion; and adult criminal behavior (Plomin et al., 1990). Researchers consistently state that a genetic propensity does not mean that the behavior is destined by heredity.

Parents and children tend to share their biological heredity and their environments. Therefore, in family studies, it is difficult to distinguish one from the other. Behavioral geneticists typically study twins reared apart or adopted children to differentiate effects of family environment from genetic factors.

Genograms, discussed later in this book, are an important tool for describing a person's genetic history and are an essential part of most social histories (Bernhardt & Rauch, 1993; McGoldrick et al., 1999).

Social Networks

Humans start life with their family systems as their primary social networks, except in those cases where infants or children have no family environment, as when they are raised in group or institutional care. As humans mature, they typically come into contact with an increasingly diverse network of social relationships. Even in infancy and early childhood, they are influenced by the social networks of which their caregivers are a part. Social networks include people who share proximate space and interact socially with the person on a regular basis, such as friends, neighbors, classmates, coworkers, teammates, professionals who provide services to the person, and members of faith or civic organizations with which the person is affiliated.

The mastery of social skills, that is, the capacity to relate positively to others, occurs through interaction with family and social networks. Social skills are affected by the way a person thinks and feels about other people. To the extent that social environments nurture and support the child, the child will learn self-worth, competence, and trust. If the environments are hostile or confusing, children learn behaviors that may be harmful to themselves or others, such as withdrawal or aggression. Of course, few environments are uniformly positive or negative at all times, but a general social climate tends to be consistent. Children have to learn to manage themselves across a variety of environments of increasingly complexity as they mature. In the United States, the age at which children enter more complex environments has dropped significantly. Child Trends reports increasing rates of children in out-of-home care at young ages (Child Trends DataBank, 2005). In 2001, 61% of children ages 0 to 6 (and not yet in kindergarten) spent time in nonparental care. Twenty-three percent were cared for by a relative, 16% by a nonrelative but in a home, and 34% in center-based programs. A focus on 2-year-olds reveals that 17% were in center-based care (up from 12% in 1995). Peer relations are thus assuming greater prominence in more children's lives at earlier ages.

Social networks are a key source of what is known as social capital, which is knowledge and resources available through relationships (Coleman, 1988). Happiness, well-being, and access to economic capital are related to personal human capital (typically measured as education and income) and social capital (typically assessed at a minimum as structure and amount of contact; Easterlin, 2000). People begin to accrue social capital early in life through their caregivers' social networks and the social environments of which they are a part. Kellam and associates (Kellam, Ling, Merisca, Brown, & Ialongo, 1998) emphasize that the social networks a person has at each stage of life set the foundation for social relations at the next stage of life.

Children are often "marginalized," that is, kept on the margins of social networks, when they are regarded as different from others. Children with disabilities, those for whom English is a second language, children of minority status, or those who have atypical behavior may face such exclusion. For example, a child who must sit in the office due to the family's religious beliefs that proscribe against parties while a class has a party may be seen as "weird" and treated differently at other times. Adults who are responsible for intentional environments, such as classrooms or structured recreational settings, must exercise skilled care to ensure that social interactions are inclusive.

Schools, neighborhoods, and the work environments of parents and other family members affect how a person develops and copes in life. The sheer amount of time children spend in child care and school environments makes these powerful social forces in human development. The quality of early care can remediate the harmful effects of a home life challenged by poverty, though the effects may not last if support outside the home diminishes as the child ages (Barnett, 1995). School quality, including quality of out-of-school programs (i.e., before-, after-, and summer school programs) exert significant effects on child outcomes (Little & Harris, 2003). Children learn academic as well as social skills through interactions with one another. Even families who homeschool their children often arrange for their children to participate in peer networks with other homeschooled children, to enable their social skills development.

As children age, they seek companionship away from home. They cluster with groups of friends and peers who share common interests. Youth who have opportunities for learning positive social interaction and civic responsibility are more likely to show competence in such areas as social communication, emotional expression, problem solving, moral judgment, and resilience in the face of adversity (Catalano, Berglund, Ryan, Lonczak, & Hawkins, 2004).

If youth are cut off from opportunities for positive youth development, they are at risk of joining gangs. Teens who spend their time in gangs may find comfort in the affinity of the group and a sense of belonging (Branch, 1997; Weiner, 1999). Unfortunately, even when the gang does not engage in negative behavior such as violence, which is often the media's focus on gangs, teens in gangs inhibit their opportunities for development by restricting their social interactions. They may find that later in life, when they are living more independently, they are unprepared to live with typical social challenges.

In adulthood, people tend to participate in many chosen and given social networks. Most people are employed and regard certain coworkers as members of their social networks. They may belong to faith communities, friendship circles, groups of shared interest (such as hiking clubs or quilting circles), or they may just gather together informally at regular places such as pubs or parks.

People increasingly participate in social networks through electronic media rather than face-to-face contact. They communicate through cell phones and other handheld communications devices and online networks such as "MySpace.com," which facilitates personalized communications or "eharmony.com," which is a matchmaking service. For people who have resources (i.e., the capacity to purchase equipment and services for electronic communications), electronic media create opportunities for individuals to have large and diverse networks, although caution must be exercised to practice appropriate security measures and minimize risk of exposure to exploitive relationships in such relatively open arenas.

In addition to media that facilitate two-way or multiple participant communication, the mass media transmit one-way messages about social norms to viewers and listeners. The ubiquitous messenger of mass culture is, of course, television. People of all ages watch a huge number of hours of television programming each week. Children who watch limited hours of educational programs appropriate for their age level acquire certain school readiness skills while those who watch cartoons or entertaining shows do more poorly on indicators of academic success (MacBeth, 1996). The American Academy of Pediatrics (2006) recommends that total television time be limited to no more than 1 to 2 hours per day and that parents restrict programming to nonviolent, educational shows suitable for the child's age. The huge popularity of electronic media and their effectiveness in helping people of all ages feel connected to one another is without dispute. What is unknown is what effect electronic media will have on the general well-being of humankind, because human history has never seen such a phenomenon and thus far it has existed for only a few decades.

The Individual, Families, and Social Networks

As a person's social history emerges, the story about who is in the history and how the person related to and continues to relate to other people typically forms the heart of the story. Human service professionals listen to histories with awareness that strong families protect members from harm, teach values and healthy behaviors, and provide support through hard times. Families teach social skills like communication, problem solving, cooperation, moral decision making, and spiritual awareness. They can provide a foundation for each member's self-esteem, happiness, creativity, and cultural and ethnic identity. Fragile or conflicted families can teach members to distrust others and feel vulnerable. They may relate to others in ways that are hostile, exploitive, or detached. The extent to which this foundation is realized in other social relations depends on the nature of the person's informal and formal social networks, which can reinforce or hinder the person's inclinations.

Communities and Organizations

Social relationships and networks are the media through which individuals relate to their communities and the organizations of which they are a part. People tend to be affiliated with multiple communities and organizations.

Communities

Communities may be those based on location (e.g., where they now live or formerly lived or where they work or study), experience (such as communities of war veterans, survivors of cancer, school alumni, or ex-offenders), or interest (such as people who are affiliated as artists, rap musicians, genealogy buffs, or followers of a certain religion). Communities, which may be formally or informally organized, can be described structurally by such indicators as boundaries (what indicates who is in and who is not) and number and characteristics of members. They may also be described functionally, which typically would include indicators of shared activities, resources, cohesion among members, and quality of relations with people outside the community.

This discussion will focus on the influence of geographic communities because the next section on the broader environment will essentially address dynamics of how communities of experience and interest might influence human social development.

Any thorough life history review will include a good description and interpretation of the communities in which the person has lived. Geographic communities vary according to several factors in the physical, social, and economic environments. People who live in substandard housing with no toilet facilities, go to bed each night anticipating that they may hear gunfire, attend poor quality schools, drink polluted water, face recurring natural disasters, or grow accustomed to political corruption have significantly different histories than those who live in gated communities with manicured lawns, fiddle with excessive electronic gadgetry in every room, access emergency medical assistance in less than 4 minutes, and feel so safe they leave their doors unlocked at all hours.

Researchers are just beginning to understand how and to what degree geographic communities influence individual development. The relationship is complex, mediated by family factors as well as historical, cultural, economic, and other characteristics of the community (Brooks-Gunn, Duncan, & Aber, 1997). Individuals tend to relate to a relatively small geographic area. In urban communities, that would be a block or neighborhood; in rural areas, it might be an area along a particular highway or around a cluster of homes or a convenience store. These small areas are embedded in somewhat larger communities, which are in towns or districts of cities, and so on. Within these areas, individuals find resources and opportunities for engaging in or refraining from certain social behaviors. A community's assets and processes affect how a person behaves socially.

The relational processes among residents in a community convey the social norms of the community (Garner & Raudenbush, 1991). People tend to act in accordance with social norms. For example, where youth are expected to finish high school, as communicated by multiple messages from peers, parents, neighbors, faith and business leaders, and mass media, graduation rates are higher. Where educational norms are ambivalent or lacking, as when adults are relatively silent about expectations or harshly critical of schools, youth seem less motivated to finish.

Chapter 6 contains guides for profiling communities according to indicators of population, geography, housing, economy, education, health and safety, and an array of other factors. Such profiles, including asset mapping (assets may be people, natural resources, physical structures, businesses, educational settings, or informal organizations; see Community Tool Box, 2006; Kretzmann & McKnight, 1993).

Regions of the United States, such as New England, the Deep South, and the Northwest, have characteristics that differentiate them from one another, although increased relocations among them and common media and markets are reducing their distinctiveness, just as globalization has tended to blend international cultures. Yet differences persist, and within regions, subregions, even neighborhoods, variations persist. For example, where textile mills once flourished in the South, mill owners often constructed rental housing, which eventually was sold to employees. These "mill villages" had a common culture since every family had at least one, often several, wage earning employees at the mill. When the mills died, the villages remained and transformed into various new communities with vestiges of the old culture still present. In the Project on Human Development in Chicago Neighborhoods, Felton Earls and his associates have tracked the evolution of neighborhoods that were predominantly Anglo American, then African American, then Hispanic (Earls, 1999). The characteristics of the area changed as each group became dominant.

Poverty tends to be linked to geography. Material deprivation may vary among children living within a neighborhood, but in many areas, the entire neighborhood is deprived. The notion of an "underclass" that lives in such areas refers to people affected by (1) persistent and intergenerational transmission of poverty; (2) geographic concentration; (3) social isolation from mainstream society; (4) unemployment and underemployment; (5) low skills and education; and, often (6) membership in a minority group (Brooks-Gunn, Klebanov, & Liaw, 1995; Gephart & Brooks-Gunn, 1997, p. xiv). Research has found that children in neighborhoods without these deprived characteristics are more likely to have better developmental outcomes (e.g., in terms of health, behavior, contentment; Leventhal & Brooks-Gunn, 2000). This holds true for children whose parents came from deprived areas and moved to more endowed neighborhoods—somehow, the children benefit from the surrounding resources (Gephart, 1997). Still, while neighborhoods do exert an effect, it is mild. What most predicts the differences between children who do well and those who do poorly is related to family processes (such as more than one stable parent and parental employment) and their own individual characteristics (such as intelligence, capacity to handle stress).

When an individual makes an inadequate adjustment to a culture different from the one of his or her origin, the results can be tragic. In one situation, a young Euro American gay man, survivor of extreme physical and sexual abuse in a fundamentalist religious household, raised in a small southern mill town that condemned his sexual orientation, moved to Los Angeles. There he was regarded as a "hillbilly," a term he resented because, in southern mill towns, it is a derogatory term reserved for people who live in Appalachia, not the mill territories. Without the external restrictions inherent in his social environment of origin, he felt lost and confused, and experimented with a variety of drugs and behavior. He found himself a protector. When threatened with rejection by his protector, he went on a drinking and drug binge and assaulted the woman next door, who reminded him of his mother. Such cultural factors as regional religious fundamentalism, attitudes toward homosexuality, southern white mill town culture in transition, and difficulty in adjusting to a new community are critical to understanding his behavior.

Social environments vary geographically. Thus an individual's or family's social history must be assessed with attention to the various locations in which the history occurred.

Organizations

Humans live in interaction with multiple formal and informal organizations. Organizations include such groups as schools, hospitals, sports leagues, synagogues, banks, restaurants, listservs, libraries, city councils, corporations, political parties, waste management companies, and hundreds of other groups that make up communities and society. Organizations range from small, informal groups such as book clubs to large international conglomerates such as the International Red Cross or the Sony Corporation. The influence is reciprocal; humans influence organizations and are influenced by them.

Humans relate to organizations in multiple ways. They may be part of the internal processes of the organization as leaders or workers. They may be consumers such as students, patients, or customers. They may be sponsors, such as older taxpayers who support schools or donors to nonprofit organizations. On a typical day, any one person is directly and indirectly influenced by multiple organizations.

A rather massive knowledge base has revealed considerable information about how organizations function to influence human social development and well-being (see, e.g., Anderson, Ones, Sinangil, & Viswesvaran, 2002; Poelmans, 2005; Schneider & Smith, 2004). In general, studies have differentiated governmental, business, and nonprofit organizations. Structurally, organizations can be described in terms of their governance, leadership, facilities, strategic planning and management, resources, marketing, teamwork, external alliances, and results. Functionally, they are often described in terms of relationships among people within the organization and relationships among those within and outside the organizations. Studies of organizational climate and culture have identified those organizational factors that affect the people associated with the organization (Lindahl, 2006; Orpinas & Horne, 2006). Within the organization, such factors as trust, morale, communication, decision-making processes, leader credibility, inclusion, equity, benefits, and conflict management are related to participant well-being, whether they are employees, volunteers, stakeholders, or consumers. External relations are affected by such factors as consumer satisfaction, adaptability, accountability, image, and ethical decision making.

How organizations influence individuals and vice versa can be assessed in multiple ways. For example, with regard to school environments, students, teachers, administrators, and parents are more engaged if schools have smaller student enrollments, small classes, integrative curricula, and organizational decision-making processes that enable students and teachers to influence how they "live and learn" (Seidman, Aber, & French, 2004). While school is the work of the young, eventually most people enter employment to garner the financial resources necessary to sustain their lives and pursue happiness. How people feel about their work will affect their home lives, and vice versa. Workers are more effective if they are supported by organizations that empower them through an organizational climate that enables mutual trust, common goals, and continuous learning (Gutierrez, Parsons, & Cox, 1998). Groups like the Families and Work Institute (n.d.) have promoted supportive policies such as family leave, health care benefits, vacation time, release time for school meetings, flex time, and other alternatives to help people manage stress and balance their work and family lives effectively (Vannoy & Dubeck, 1998; Williams, 2000).

The social history will include themes about the person's organizational affiliations, how closely affiliated the person was with the organization, the person's regard for the organization's values and mission, and the dynamics that affected the person's association with the organization. For example, a person may have been raised in a children's home. The professional who is assessing the social history will be able to do so more thoroughly with knowledge of such factors as whether the children's home met quality standards, suffered any turmoil such as sexual abuse allegations, received any accreditation or awards, had low staff turnover and stable strong leadership, and other relevant factors. Information about each organization in the history, such as quality school indicators, how termination decisions were made when an employer downsized, morale in a National Guard unit, and a host of other indicators, can reveal insight into the facts and meaning of the person's life.

Formal organizational assessments may be an important part of an individual or family social history. The assessment may be qualitative, such as gathering interview information about a focused topic, or quantitative, based on a rating system. Tools to facilitate the assessment are generally tailored to particular purposes, such as assessing psychosocial factors related to school climate, health and safety, or readiness for change. For example, the Centers for Disease Control, National Institute for Occupational Health and Safety (2006) maintains an inventory of source information about organizational assessment tools. Many other tools can be accessed by searching for specific topics such as school climate assessment or workplace safety assessment.

A thorough social history will use various means to examine key factors associated with the most salient organizations and communities in the life of the person or family that is the subject of the history.

Social Ecology: The Broader Environment

Everyone's life history is affected by their position in society, which is related to such culturally ascribed characteristics as gender, ethnicity, social class, age, sexual identity, religion, globalization, and governmental policies that affect family life. Society is socially constructed through the medium of culture. Starting at an early age, humans learn to think about the world through language that is shared with other members of the culture. Throughout life, social interactions influence a person's constantly changing perceptions. How people regard their own and others' characteristics is shaped by attributions learned from other people. Collectively, the shared perceptions form what is known as culture.

Culture, Class, Race-Ethnicity, and National Origin

Culture, traditionally the domain of anthropologists, is now recognized as a powerful force by all social and behavioral scientists. Culture, the systematic organization of social behavior through customs, beliefs, and values, pervades all life and significantly affects human development (See, 1998; Super & Harkness, 1999). D'Andrade and Strauss (1992) observe that what a person does on a typical day is influenced by a shared system of understandings about the appropriate things to do. Each individual affiliates with several cultures (e.g., by racial-ethnic identity, religion, national identity, socioeconomic class, gender identity, and occupation). Culture is transmitted from generation to generation through familial roles, communication patterns, emotional expression, personal control, individualism, collectivism, spirituality, and religiosity (Betancourt & Lopez, 1993; Santisteban, 2002). At times an individual or family faces conflicting loyalties between cultures, as when they migrate to a different country, marry across racial-ethnic groups, or move upward or downward in socioeconomic class. If managed poorly, this tension can breed conflict and dysfunction.

Historically, race was regarded as a biological characteristic, but that notion has been discounted. Based on a review of scientific evidence, Smedley and Smedley (2005, p. 16) declared, "Race as biology is fiction, racism as a social problem is real," though the myth persists that race is biologically determined. People do have a wide range of physical attributes that are biologically determined, but whether the attributes are ascribed to a particular "race" is a social construct. Thus, people who identify as "black" may have a wide range of skin colors and hair types. Smedley and Smedley reiterate, as many social scientists have done, that race is a social construction, nested in ethnicity, that is based on perceived differences among cultures. Members of an ethnic group share a common culture and common ancestry, country/region of origin, and/or group history (Santisteban, 2002). Ethnic identity is generally a source of pride, but historic differences in power among ethnic groups have generated feelings of shame in some members of oppressed groups and elitism in privileged groups. How a person identifies ethnically and the regard he or she has for the ethnic group significantly affects his or her well-being. Similarly, the disdain or hatred members of one group may feel for another breeds conflict and war.

The complex process of acculturation occurs when immigrant groups change their attitudes and behaviors toward a dominant group with a different culture (Booth & Crouter, 1997; Burnett & Thompson, 2005). These transitions create tension for the individual and the family. The meeting of cultural groups occurs under varying circumstances; in many cases, immigrants come from war-torn, oppressed areas, and the migration process itself is traumatic. When children migrate separately from their parents, they are particularly at risk for problems (Bemak & Greenberg, 1994). Even people who migrate under positive conditions, for example, in response to a business opportunity, must adapt. The dominant culture often looks down on the immigrant's culture. Studies of immigrants have demonstrated varying styles of adaptation, some of which can induce harmful negative effects on children. They may be marginalized (feel identity with no group), withdrawn (try to maintain separate identity), assimilated (reject culture of origin), or integrated (able to balance bicultural identities). These are not states but processes that elicit stress as they occur.

Privileges and disadvantages are not evenly distributed across the human population. The power to affect one's own life and the lives of others is generally linked to socioeconomic class—those with wealth and privilege related to favored social positions, such as a particular ethnicity or gender, have relatively more power than those in less favored positions. Margaret Wetherell (1996) observed that

> power is intimately connected with social identity in the sense that people's place in a system of social organization has a large bearing on the resources they can command, and on whether attempts to secure power are seen as reasonable and appropriate or as disruptive and illegitimate. (p. 315)

Historically, the use of physical force has assured those in power that they will be secure in their positions. They control such resources as law enforcement, the judiciary, the military, banks, and other institutions of power. Force need not be imminently present or used. Over time, social norms, backed by the potential for force, help keep people in their social positions.

Income and social class are not the same. Income fluctuates and generally rises in a family over a typical child's life, except in cases of persistent poverty. Generally, a family's social and economic positions are determined not simply by income but also by parents' educational level, occupational status, and assets (e.g., property ownership). In some cultures, class mobility occurs. People can gain access to power and resources and shift their social positions, or lose their privileged positions.

A British study of 30,000 children over the course of their development from birth to adulthood found that persistent and accumulating experiences of socioeconomic disadvantage throughout childhood and adolescence had a significant negative effect on adult competencies (Schoon et al., 2002). Similar studies in the United States have shown that regardless of social class, a family's low income during a child's earliest years predicts lower academic achievement by the child in later years (Duncan, Yeung, Brooks-Gunn, & Smith, 1998). Public policies that help children compensate for socioeconomic disadvantage promote children's gaining a fairer chance for getting out of poverty as they mature.

A history of oppression, that is, exposure to aggression by dominant groups, tends to generate protective practices in oppressed groups. Individuals become keenly attuned to subtle cues in interactions. They adapt in ways that reduce the perceived threat, such as compliance, avoidance, or subversion. For example, the subculture of poverty that exists when low-income families are crowded together in poor neighborhoods supports suspicion and opposition to the dominant culture (Brooks-Gunn et al., 1997). In these areas, law enforcement officers are likely to be feared rather than trusted and respected. People may prepare to defend themselves with force if threatened. Gangs provide a source of security. Sometimes, behaviors that helped individuals adjust to difficult cultural transitions become dysfunctional in other contexts. For example, carrying a concealed weapon may be important for protecting oneself and one's loved ones when a gang war is under way in a community. Carrying that weapon into a predominantly middle-class neighborhood of people from the dominant culture may provoke harsh penalties.

Culture, race-ethnicity, and socioeconomic status powerfully affect the social environments of humans as they develop. Individuals, singly and collectively, also affect the social environment. In a society committed to equality, acknowledging a legacy of oppression and offering supports to individuals and groups from historically oppressed populations will help to even the unfair odds.

Gender Identity and Gender Roles

Aside from a few obvious differences between males and females (reproductive organs, body hair, average body size), much of what is regarded as "male" or "female" is socially constructed and culturally influenced by prevailing ideologies of gender role stereotypes and norms (Bem, 1993). In many ways, people learn to be male or female and develop an identity that they are male or female. Yet their practice of behaviors that are culturally regarded as masculine or feminine varies widely, whether they identify as male or female. Each culture has its own regard for gender roles. In the United States, tradition regarded men as breadwinners, protectors, builders and repairers, and decision makers. Women were nurturers, resource managers, peacemakers, and organizers. These normative gender roles influence individual life decisions about such critical matters as education, mate selection, family formation, and the aging process (Adler, 2001; Satow, 2001). These notions persist, although they have been broadly challenged, to be replaced by current contradictions about what roles are generally expected based on gender.

At the turn of the 21st century, people in developed countries such as the United States are generally experiencing ambivalence about what it means to be a man. Maleness is not simply biological; it is social. Men learn how to be men (i.e., what to wear, how to look, how to act) from men and women in their lives, but their essential identity tends to come from their relations to one another (Connell, 1995; Zilbergeld, 1992).

Thus, a son's relationship to his father (present or absent) or father-figure exerts a powerful effect on his identity, development, and adult behavior. Even men who hated their fathers tend to be like them. Increasingly, boys are being raised without consistent access to a male father figure, which can create identity confusion (Tamis-LaMonda & Cabrera, 2002).

The process is similar for women. Conventionally, female meant being nurturing, compassionate, sexy, self-sacrificing, and submissive. These characteristics have been valued less than traditional male characteristics, as evidenced by failure to compensate for jobs requiring these traits. Historically, women were punished for being independent, aggressive, or dominant, though now the "new woman" ideology expects her to be assertive, self-sufficient, rational, and competitive (Philpot, Brooks, Lusterman, & Nutt, 1997). Women struggle with perceived pressure to "do it all" (Kite, 2001).

These changing roles started after World War II and escalated throughout the latter part of the 20th century, so most young people today have been exposed to these gender role conflicts. Put confused males and confused females together in marital and co-parenting roles, and the result is an epidemic of family discord. Men and women argue, physically fight, get depressed, separate, divorce, and try again with someone else but remain at risk of dissatisfaction with their relationships with the opposite sex. Children exposed to this discord can suffer developmentally. Marriage rates have dropped precipitously in recent years. For example, in 1970, the median age at first marriage was 20.8 years for women and 23.2 years for men (Fields & Casper, 2001). By 2000, these ages had risen to 25.1 years and 26.8 years, respectively. People's inclination to marry or make other forms of lasting social commitment is declining.

Each person's social history will include stories about how men and women relate within the person's family and social networks. In contemporary relationships women and men may share expectations of one another, such as agreeing that "he will rock the baby at night because he is a nurturing father." Or they may disagree, such as when she expects him to rock the baby but he believes "men don't do that—I need my sleep so I can provide for the family." Or they may be confused, struggling to find ways to develop reliable expectations. They may agree to be traditional, with the mother taking full responsibility except in rare circumstances when she needs help. The key to a successful relationship is communication about gender roles and all expectations. A thorough social history will examine such gender-related factors as the person's beliefs about what it means to be a man or woman, how activities inside and outside the home are organized according to gender, and how various people express emotions and power.

Sexuality and Reproduction

Cultural norms about gender also influence the expression of sexuality and sexual orientation. Typically, people will develop a gender identity as male or female and a general sexual orientation that is heterosexual (i.e., they feel sexual attraction to the opposite sex), homosexual (they feel sexual attraction to the same sex), or bisexual (their sexual attraction is to either sex). Some individuals have a complex gender identity and regard themselves as transsexual—that is, they live in a gendered body but adopt the typical gender roles and mannerisms of the opposite sex. Yet none of these categories seem to be fixed because sexuality is multidimensional and changes with context (Rothblum, 2000). Sexual behavior (the type of sexual activity practiced by the individual), sexual identity (self-identified masculine or feminine gender identity and sexual orientation identity), and sexual desire (feelings of attraction and arousal) can vary over time and from one context to another (Peplau & Garnets, 2000). In general, women are more likely than men to expect an emotional relationship and partner-centered orientation in their sexual relations (Peplau & Garnets, 2000). Sexuality may be a means to intimacy, but it may also be an expression of objectifying or exploiting another person. Clear communication and mutual choice are the keys to healthy sexual interaction.

Each culture practices norms that influence how sexuality is expressed. Prevailing discriminatory norms in the United States recognize heterosexuality as the preferred sexual orientation and support a rigid social hierarchy that treats people with other sexual orientations as subordinate. Tolerance for homosexuality has increased considerably in the past two decades, but homophobia is still rampant, as the recent state-by-state effort to outlaw same-sex marriage has indicated (Garnets & Peplau, 2000). Sexuality can be a critical means to pleasure and life satisfaction, but when people face criticism from their families, neighbors, and the broader society, their right to happiness can be impaired. Their sexual identity is also affected by pervasive media messages that portray stylized images of thin, muscular young people engaged in certain types of presumably pleasurable sexual interactions. These images are impossible for most people to follow as models, so they are disappointed in themselves. Dangerously, many of the images are blended with violence, creating an impression of tolerance for forced sexual relations.

Hyde and Jaffee (2000) observe that studies indicate children first experience sexual fantasies and attractions at about age 10, boys begin masturbating at about age 12, and girls are most likely to first experience sex in relations with boys, starting masturbation later. As many as 25% of girls report their first sexual intercourse was unwanted and 4% say it was forced (Laumann, Gagnon, Michael, & Michaels, 1994). People thus may learn to associate fear, anger, shame, or disappointment with sexuality, rather than joy or contentment. They may develop sexual dysfunction, which can induce emotional effects that spill into other areas of their lives (Leiblum & Rosen, 1988).

The sexual history overlaps with the history of intimate relationships (addressed in the attachment domain) and reproduction. While some cultures still support "love, marriage, baby carriage" as the preferred sequence of events, reality involves many diverse steps to reproduction (Pallone, 2003). Some people start with careful selection of a committed mate while others cognitively separate sexual intercourse from its consequences and deal with the effects as they occur (Feingold, 1992). Childbearing may result from careful planning and spacing of each pregnancy, or serendipitous pregnancy following unprotected sex. Individuals or couples can rely on technology such as sperm banks, fertility drugs, surrogate parenting, and in vitro fertilization to facilitate their reproduction when they choose (Rosen, 2005). People now recognize the grief of a miscarried pregnancy. Elective abortion can prevent the medical or psychological crises of unwanted pregnancy. Adoption can ease the despair of infertile couples or single individuals who yearn to be parents. Even though people have multiple reproductive choices in the postmodern world, the process of starting a new life is laden with emotion. How a person's biological parents conceived the person has significant meaning for most people. Likewise, how the person and his or her partner make reproductive decisions reveals much about the person.

Taking a sexual history is an important part of any social history, though it can be difficult because people typically desire privacy about their sexuality and, in a culture that can be harshly judgmental, they may be sensitive about whether they will be criticized or deemed inadequate in some way. The very language of sexuality can be challenging, given that people tend to use slang or euphemistic words and to misunderstand anatomical terms. Families often have sexual secrets that are well protected, so asking questions may be threatening. History takers must be specifically trained and prepared to ask questions sensitively about potentially embarrassing or painful topics and to use various language tools that are culturally and situationally appropriate (see, e.g., Donahey, 2004; Skelton & Matthews, 2001; Watson, 2002).

Spirituality and Religion

A person's beliefs about transcendent forces constitute the essence of his or her spirituality. Spiritual faith influences how people form values and construct meaning from life events, particularly those events that have to do with profound transitions, such as death or tragic misfortune (Canda, 1998; Coles, 1990). Belief in forces that transcend human experience helps people to find hope when life challenges them with agony or fear (Martin & Martin, 2003).

Such beliefs can also inspire motivation to pursue fulfillment and optimal use of talents. People use the term "have faith" in encouraging one another to pursue their dreams.

Religion is an organized system that addresses beliefs about morality and powers beyond humanity. Religious communities promote spirituality, although people experience spirituality without religion, too. Furthermore, people can practice religious traditions without experiencing spirituality.

For some people, religion and/or spirituality exert vital, even dominant, influences in their lives. They organize their daily lives according to religious expectations, including how they eat, dress, behave, consume, work, socialize, serve others, and participate in religious activities. Some people regard their faith as a more subtle constant presence in their lives. For others, their religious orientation affects life rituals, such as recognitions of birth, marriage, or death, and otherwise has no major influence on their ways of life.

While most people find that their spirituality and religion strengthen their capacity to manage life, some develop serious problems related to religious abuse or maladaptive uses of religious practices (Artuerburn & Felton, 2001). People may also develop an addiction to religion, using religious practices to control interaction with others (Booth, 1991). *Religious abuse* refers to psychological or other injuries that occur when religious leaders with authority, including parents, manipulate followers to increase their own power and control. They may use physical coercion, sexual abuse, or psychological intimidation, such as condemnation. The pairing of such abusive behavior with their religious authority induces severe spiritual and mental trauma in the victim. *Ritualistic abuse* is a severe form of religious abuse that occurs as part of a religious rite, such as beating someone during a religious service as punishment for sin or raping or killing someone as part of a supposed rite.

A person's social history will reflect the religious and spiritual practices and traditions of the family's social network (Miller, 2005). When assessing a person's religious or spiritual history, studies have typically examined four dimensions: public participation (e.g., attending services), affiliation (e.g., belonging to a religious group), private religious practices (e.g., prayer, meditation), and religious coping (turning to religion when faced with a problem; George, Ellison, & Larson, 2002).

Government and Public Policy

In the United States, formal resources to support healthy human development are embedded in an intricate system of public and private institutions that operate at local, state, and federal levels. The overarching principles behind the system are embedded in the legal framework of the nation, with its focus on individual rights in relation to the government, and a free market economy. Still, the states and local governments have considerable flexibility in determining how local societies will operate. The focus here is on public action that targets the promotion of healthy, prosocial human development.

Each state can develop its own resources, although the federal government provides incentives and requirements that strongly influence what states and localities do. For example, each local economy is different but depends on regulatory actions by the federal government. Each locality develops its own voting procedures, within state and federal regulations. Generally, policies related to human development are enacted in response to identified problems that are identified through participative political processes. Recent major issues, for example, include access to affordable health care, availability of affordable quality child care, disparities in school funding, racial-ethnic profiling, and voting exclusion. How each of these is resolved from one area to another will affect the quality of life for residents.

Communities typically offer an array of health, education, and human services. These include, but are not limited to the following:

- Public assistance programs (e.g., Temporary Assistance to Needy Families (TANF), Food Stamps)
- Emergency assistance (e.g., from private agencies for food, shelter, clothing, payment of utility bills, house repair)
- Housing assistance
- Child welfare systems (protective services, foster care, adoption)

- Family services (e.g., counseling, family life education, budget advice)
- Out-of-home care resources for children
- Education system (preschool, primary and secondary, higher education)
- Mental health care system
- Drug or alcohol treatment system
- Health care system
- Elder care system
- Disabilities or special needs services system
- Cultural resources (e.g., art, music, drama)
- Recreational resources
- Victim services system
- Family court (e.g., child support, divorce) system
- Law enforcement system
- Juvenile justice system
- Criminal justice system

Sooner or later, most people's lives are significantly influenced by several of these systems. The quantity and quality of a person's "system involvement" is an important part of the social history.

Amazingly, even with a vast network of formal resources, individual and family needs often go unmet. People may encounter barriers for reasons related to access (e.g., no transportation, conflict with work hours), affordability, eligibility restrictions, or cultural relevance. Or the system may have gaps, with no resources to address the unique needs of a particular situation. The number of people who need the resource may exceed the response capacity of the provider. The quality of the resources, particularly the skill of providers, may be deficient. Assuring that formal systems do adequately support human development is a continual governance and management process.

People's social histories reveal the ways in which they have related to their governments. This includes not only access to and use of resources provided by the government and involvement in various systems, but also participation in government, such as voting, participating in campaigns, expressing opinions, or serving on decision-making bodies.

Globalization

Anyone living in the 21st century experiences the opportunities and risks that have emerged as globalization sweeps across the planet. Historically, people have identified with their cultural groups and the nation-states of which they are a part. Increasingly, their identities are changing as communications and economic markets penetrate the political boundaries of nations, creating transnational social relationships and exchanges. Whereas citizens of the United States claim the identity "American," people of other North American and South American countries now say, "We are all Americans—you are people of the USA." National identity is less salient, as people often relate to the multinational corporations that employ them or to nongovernmental organizations (NGOs) such as Doctors Without Borders, Greenpeace, or faith-based missions.

Globalization has produced a large, rapid transnational flow of people, ideas, products, and cultural norms. The interactions have yielded increased empowerment and positive well-being, but they have also induced exploitation. People move across political borders for reasons of economic opportunity as temporary or resident workers or immigrants planning to relocate. They also move as refugees from war and civil conflict, slaves, and occupation forces. Globalization has enabled the development of productive networks of artists, health care providers, and people of shared faith but it has also spawned networks of terrorists, drug dealers, and human traffickers. The market and communication factors in globalization have evolved so rapidly that international governmental, business, and nonprofit organizations are scrambling to develop means to protect human rights and regulate practices for the good of the world's people and environment (Brysk, 2002).

The impact of globalization on human development and everyday social life has yet to be adequately studied. Demographic studies show that people in the United States are more likely now than in the past to live near people whose culture and national origin is different from their own. People have more diverse choices with regard to food, consumer goods, music, and other cultural experiences (Hannerz, 2000). Educational systems have adapted to accommodate more languages and more advanced curricula to promote competitiveness with people from other countries in the global marketplace. Local job opportunities are linked to decisions of multinational corporations. People have variously celebrated the increasing diversity or resisted it through nationalistic and ethno-centric organizations such as the American Border Patrol (an anti-immigration group).

People's social histories are affected by how they perceive their identities—including their understanding of how they came to be who and where they are—and social relationships within this rapidly emerging transnational context. Even if their global awareness is limited, the type and extent of resources in their social environments will be affected by various global forces that may be distinct for each community.

The social ecology that surrounds an individual's life over time affects whether the person thrives, survives, or declines. Understanding a person's social history requires knowledge about the unique characteristics of his or her various social environments over time.

Individuals in the Social Environment

In the eternal debate about free will versus determinism, most contemporary social scientists come to the opinion that both matter—the individual and environment are inextricably linked (Biddell, 1997). A person's social environment may determine many factors that influence the person's life. Yet the person still has some degree of choice about how to respond to the environment and regulate emotions and behaviors in various contexts. By exercising human agency, individuals actively pursue goals within the environments of which they are a part. They adapt to environments and they also influence the environments, causing changes in the environment that affect themselves and others. Thus all lives are interlinked.

People can actively create their own social lives and influence their own outcomes and social positions, within limits. Social structures and processes constrain individual choice by affecting opportunities, threats, privileges, and deprivations. Individuals can chart their own courses within certain prescribed boundaries. The boundaries vary from one individual and group to another. Some boundaries are real while others are believed to be real by the affected individuals. For example, women who seek to advance to management or corporate leadership positions may encounter real barriers to advancement in organizations where the leadership structure is intolerant of a significant female presence. Women in such organizations seek advancement and are rejected for unfair reasons. Other organizations may be more open to women's advancement, and yet women hesitate to try to advance based on the assumption that they will be rebuffed. Those who try move forward fairly. Women in the former organization face real barriers; those in the latter perceive barriers that may not be present.

Whether people perceive that they have freedom to choose or a degree of control over their own lives significantly affects social behavior (Bandura, 1977, 1997). People construct their own identities, or sense of self, based on their social experiences. Part of this sense of self is a generalized sense of personal efficacy, the belief that they can achieve the change they desire. This belief, variously called willpower, motivation, agency, self-determination, and other terms, is the spark that stimulates individual action within social settings. Perceived efficacy varies from one situational context to another. Essentially, a person feels more confident of being efficacious in some settings than in others. Some people are more comfortable on a sports field than in a boardroom or in a church sanctuary than in a deep forest, or vice versa, depending on where they feel a greater sense of efficacy.

People bring their beliefs about their personal efficacy and abilities to different social situations. They have a propensity to act in a certain way based on these beliefs and abilities. Whether they behave according to their propensity depends on situational factors (Rotter, 1982) that elicit certain behaviors from individuals and inhibit others. For example, a person who has the capacity for empathy with the suffering of others may not actively show compassion until confronted with a situation where someone is in need of help, such as seeing someone gasp for breath in a public setting and providing first aid or calling for emergency medical assistance. The national call for community service is based on awareness that creating opportunities for people to show care leads them to find even more situations where they can help others, thus building a stronger, more interactive society. From a different perspective, social control strategies such as mandatory arrest of domestic violence perpetrators seek to inhibit negative behaviors by assuring negative consequences for harmful behavior (Buzawa & Buzawa, 1996; Gelles, 1993). Whether the laws actually do change the situation and deter the behavior depends on many factors associated with the individuals, situation, and context. Presumably, when people know with a degree of certainty that they will be arrested if they commit an act of violence, it will deter their behavior. The situational context is different from areas where arrest almost never follows the assault, and thus the rates of the behavior are lower, at least for people who care about getting arrested.

Self-efficacy affects how people perceive themselves and act in social settings (Bandura, 1997, 2002). Greater self-efficacy is associated with higher levels of life satisfaction. People try to explain their own success or failure. People who cope well seem to attribute their success and failures to their own efforts. People who cope maladaptively tend to see their success or failure as matters of luck or forces beyond their control.

Collective efficacy occurs when groups of people unite to seek a change in their environment (Duncan, Duncan, & Okut, 2003; Watson, Chemers, & Preiser, 2001). They recognize the limitations of individual efficacy and join forces to pursue their goals. Even when people appraise their situations realistically and realize the limits of their capacity to change the environment, their well-being can be affected by the hope that somehow the situation and the environment will change positively (McGeer, 2004). People with little or no hope are at risk of depression and despair that drains their will to influence the environment.

Through personal efficacy, collective efficacy, and hope, people try to make sense of the world around them and integrate that into their future anticipations and behaviors (Wetherell, 1996). In some cases, life has given them such contradictory messages that they feel fragmented, lost, and confused. For example, research on maltreated children indicates they tend to misattribute other people's intentions, believing, for example, that someone can be trusted when in fact that person is exploitive (Dodge, Bates, & Pettit, 1990; also see various chapters in Meyers et al., 2002). Therapeutic programs for at-risk youth often train them to assess and respond to situations more realistically.

As people exert influences on their immediate environments, they do so as parts of a greater context. Actions that look personal are often part of a greater social movement, though the process may not be immediately obvious. Giele (1998) studied the 1950s phenomenon of women entering the paid workforce in the United States. She found four main motivations that affected the choices of women who were among the first to seek careers outside the home: new moral belief in the egalitarian roles of men and women, economic necessity, pursuit of improved well-being and life satisfaction, and desire to cope with perceived uncertainty about the future. In each case, the individuals assessed factors in their environment and made personal choices regarding their own life situations. Each woman's action changed her own immediate environment whether she achieved her personal goal or not. What resulted from these multiple individual decisions was a mass movement that stimulated yet more reform, including such phenomena as the invention of more labor-saving household devices, expansion of the child care industry, reduced commitment to marriage by men and women, increased legal support for women's freedom, changing social norms regarding expectations of men and women in family life, and a host of other societal changes.

While unique individual actions may combine to form a collective change in the environment, the environment does not always produce uniform change across individuals. Many people live in the same or similar social environments, yet they behave quite differently. For example, why does one child raised in a home with a brutal father grow up to commit murder while a sibling raised in the same home never breaks the law? Why are some students in a school altruistic while others focus on self-gratification? No two social lives are exactly alike. Twins come close, but even they are different. Generally, when lives are examined closely, social environments that appear identical actually have subtle differences, and each individual brings particular perspectives and characteristics to the social situation, which makes his response unique.

The interaction of the individual with the environment is complex, affected by personal beliefs and abilities, individual differences, situational factors, and the incredible diversity of the social environment. Democratic societies support an individual's right to self-determination with due respect for others. Social history assessment enables the discovery of key patterns in how individuals have learned to exercise their own agency within and across environments.

Summary

The social life at any point in time is anything but simple. Cumulatively, over time, the person's social history reflects the dynamic interaction of various elements of the social system at all levels—family, social network, organizational affiliation, community, and society. As people develop along the predictable trajectory of human life, their social systems shift. Positive and negative life events and threatening and supportive social forces evolve around them, shaping who they become. They respond, learning and adapting as they interact, exerting influence over the social environment as their lives proceed. Capturing the essence of any particular life in a social history assessment requires an understanding of human social development within this complex, dynamic social ecological context.

4

Describing the Social History

A straightforward descriptive social history, without interpretation (discussed in the next chapter), essentially reports the facts that occurred and the meaning attributed to the events or series of events as conveyed by the key informants. This chapter covers the gathering of facts and observations that lead to such a description. The goal is to use procedures and recording methods that ensure the history is accurate, complete, and reliable.

The techniques reviewed here can be used for the most thorough histories, such as those required in an adoption study, suicide assessment, or for mitigation in criminal sentencing. Most often, the professional will require a shorter, more focused version of a social history as when developing a treatment plan for addiction, a long-term caregiving plan for an older adult, or an individualized education plan for a special needs child. The professional taking the history can extract the items, procedures, and tools that are most relevant for the purpose.

Establishing the Facts

As each human develops through time, memories, records, and artifacts are created and leave a trail of information about the life.

The professional generally relies on three sources of information to help the person bring these to the present and reconstruct the history: interviews, records, and direct observation. Each person's life history contains rich detail and a potentially massive body of information. This chapter includes several common tools used to facilitate organizing the information as it is collected.

Interviews

A social history always involves one or more interviews with the person who is the subject of the history. If the person has impaired ability to communicate due to very young age, illness, or disability, the primary informant may be someone who is a caregiver. In any case, the professional is also likely to interview someone other than the subject for purposes of validation and corroboration of facts. These informants typically include family caregivers (biological, foster, and adoptive family members or surrogates who have given primary care to the person), other kin who ever lived in the person's household as well as kin who lived elsewhere, spouses and intimate partners, neighbors, teachers, coworkers, peers, and service agency personnel.

Getting Started. An interview begins with the professional's preparation. Typically this includes developing an interview guide or protocol, which is a list of topics to cover (discussed in detail below). The interviewer needs a means of recording, which always includes paper and pen and may also include laptop computer and/or audio or visual recording equipment. Interviews require extensive note taking because they will involve short prompts from the interviewer and extended responses by the interviewee. The interviewer who is managing the communication while also recording can overlook details without the habit of careful and thorough note taking. Increasingly, professionals directly record onto computers if the use of equipment does not interfere with the client's comfort. In certain cases, making an audio or video record is relevant to the purpose of the interview, as when a professional helps a client with a terminal illness make a videotape for his or her family and posterity. The prepared professional checks to be sure the materials and equipment are ready before meeting the client.

Some professionals are reluctant to record because of concern that the note taking will interfere with the communication process. Such a concern may be more significant in the therapeutic interview. When the purpose is to take a truthful history, the record is essential to remembering the facts and assuring fidelity to the speakers' words. With experience, the recording process can become barely intrusive and may even facilitate openness by the interviewee because the note taker can choose to focus on the notepad as a way of minimizing contact, which encourages some interviewees speak more freely.

The professional will begin the interview with introductions and informal comments to create a climate of openness and comfort. Often the social history is taken within the context of a relationship that is already started. For example, the client has come for therapeutic help at a mental health program or for diagnostic assessment of a child's learning needs. Exploring the relationship would begin with a discussion of the presenting problem before the social history interview begins.

Informed Consent. The informed consent procedure, a standard professional practice, provides full disclosure about the purpose of the social history interview and asks for explicit consent. In some cases, as the history emerges, the professional may need to get additional consent from the person to contact other informants or to review records.

The purpose of taking a social history generally falls into three categories: research, personal gratification, or assessment for intervention. Of course, the purpose may encompass all three categories. The first, research, aims to document the social aspects of a person's life history to shed light on facts or theories about how lives evolve in place and time and the meaning people give to their life events. The interviewee receives the benefit of new insight into his or her history while the world of social science acquires new knowledge. Many of the books about techniques for conducting life history interviews are written for researchers (e.g., Atkinson, 1998; Denzin, 1989; Lieblich, Tuvel-Mashiach, & Zilber, 1998).

The second category, personal gratification, reflects the popular interest people seem to have for documenting their own personal and family histories. This desire seems to be universal, as the centuries of oral histories, ballads, personal art, and biographies as well as the more recent video recordings for posterity tell us. People will sometimes engage a professional to help them describe and understand their histories.

The third general purpose describes the social history as a foundation for assessment to guide intervention, such as treatment, educational approach, sentencing, or decisions about living arrangements. Such assessment is the domain of helping professionals. Describing the history is only the first step toward interpreting themes through the lens of theory and knowledge about human behavior in the social environment. The ultimate purpose aims to intervene intentionally in the trajectory of the historic patterns to break maladaptive habits or change harmful environments so that the problem is eliminated or reduced and alternative, positive factors are introduced. The intervention may be education, therapy, social control through law enforcement, or a host of other actions that actively influence the direction and nature of a social life.

From the start, the professional fully discloses the purpose of the history, what sort of record will be made, and how privacy will be protected. The interviewee has a right to know what will be done with the notes and audio or video recordings of the interview and how long the process might take. In many cases, the professional will grant the interviewee the right to review any notes or recordings that are made. In almost all situations, the professional will ask the interviewee to review the history that is written from the notes and recordings to ensure its accuracy. During the informed consent process, the professional explains any limits to confidentiality, such as the possible need to report suspected child abuse or to turn over documents to a criminal justice process under certain conditions. Professionals who represent other entities that will have access to the history, such as a multidisciplinary team, hearing officer, or judge, must disclose the relationship. The professional advises interviewees that they have the right not to answer any questions or discuss any information that they do not wish to discuss. The subject of the history should give voluntary consent for the making of the history. Informed consent essentially means the respondent is fully informed and participates by his or her own decision.

Interview Process. The quality of the interview process depends on the professional's skill as a trained communicator. Many excellent resources exist to guide development of interview skills (Atkinson, Coffey, Delamont, Lofland, & Lofland, 2001; Cormier & Cormier, 1996; Kvale, 1996; Morrison, 1993; Sattler, 1992; Weatherall, Gavey, & Potts, 2002). No written guide can substitute for supervised experience and review of one's skills through video feedback. Training will prepare the professional for the interview process, tactics to gather particular content, adaptation to various contexts, and special situations such as interviewing people with communication disorders, those with memory problems, or the involuntary client.

Detailing the qualities of a good interview process is beyond the scope of this book. In general, effective skills will facilitate building rapport and trust, encouraging accurate disclosure of facts, enabling release of feelings, and eliciting as much information as possible. The key skills involve active and reflective listening and feedback. The skilled professional will show consistent positive regard for the interviewee, nonjudgmental attitude toward the topics under discussion, and tolerance, even if the person talks about unpleasant topics or uses offensive language. Probing and requests for clarification will encourage elaborations. Careful observation of nonverbal communication such as eye contact, facial expression, and body language can yield a record of emotional expression.

Interview Guide. Most professionals will use a semistructured approach to gathering a social history. Less structure encourages client self-expression. The degree of structure will depend on the client's communication style and comfort level. Some people are characteristically reticent, others verbose. Whatever the style, the professional is likely to benefit from a set of questions or prompts to ensure coverage of comprehensive information for the social history. The person being interviewed may choose to focus on one or two topics. Without prompts from the professional, key topics could be omitted or minimized.

In clinical settings such as medical or mental health programs, the social history must often be completed as expeditiously as possible. In particular, programs that rely on managed care reimbursement must limit the amount of time with clients. The Joint Commission on Accreditation of Healthcare Organizations (JCAHO) has created standards that promote standardized approaches to assessing social histories as part of comprehensive assessments. No standard form has been widely adopted, though forms are similar across agencies. The health care field is moving toward development of a standardized electronic medical record that will include history. For other fields such as nonprofit services, criminal justice agencies, and educational settings, many companies market client record management systems that include assessment programs as part of comprehensive systems that facilitate record keeping throughout the process of assessment, services provision, outcome monitoring, and closure.

As of this writing, no standard social history guide seems to be widely used. Various programs use different forms for collecting social history information, even though clients may receive services at multiple agencies and must repeat the assessments. This may change in the future as standardized tools evolve and become more generally known. Examples of forms are included in Chapter 6.

Meanwhile, health and human services organizations are likely to have their own forms (increasingly, computer-based) to guide the social history interview. Many forms are codified to facilitate statistical compilation across multiple clients so that the forms serve program management as well as clinical purposes. The forms are likely to include sections on client identification, problems precipitating the assessment, developmental history, family composition, history of physical and mental health conditions (including disabling conditions and substance abuse), education, residential history, employment and income, legal problems, history of exposure to violence, social support networks, and social relationships with family, peers, organizations, or (for infants and children) caregivers and child care settings.

This book emphasizes the thorough collection of social history information by the independent professional. Training in thorough history taking provides a solid foundation for briefer and more focused interviews if they are required by certain settings. Thus, the tools in Chapter 6 include "Topics to Cover in a Social History Interview," a guide to gathering social history information that is as comprehensive as possible. If used in its entirety, this would require extended time, probably multiple interviews. Importantly, the guide is not intended to be a sequential list of questions! Rather, it is a checklist of topics to which the professional can refer as the interview progresses. The skilled interviewer will create appropriate questions to elicit the information and will use different questions with each interviewee, although the same topics will eventually emerge. Questions may ask for facts, such as, "When that happened, what did you do?" or feelings, such as, "When that happened, how did you feel?" Prompts may not be questions at all, such as statements that express empathy, as in, "I understand that you're saying that made you sad."

In general, the questions will move from general to more specific and from publicly known to more private and emotionally sensitive topics. For example, the interview might begin with a statement as broad as, "Tell me about yourself" or "Tell me about your family." By listening carefully to the responses, the professional will follow the lead of the client and ask the next questions. The professional's flexibility will promote the interviewee's comfort and disclosure.

Topically, the interview will cover all aspects of the person's social life. Bedrosian and Bozicas (1994, p. 24), writing about history taking with regard to families of origin, suggest the interview should meet the following purposes: (1) establishing facts about the family of origin; (2) outlining the client's development from birth onward; (3) identifying the client's basic beliefs, preferred coping strategies, information processing style, and relational habits; and (4) generating preliminary hypotheses about how the family of origin affected the client's current functioning. The family of origin, from birth through the early years, exerts a powerful influence on the person's social development, so the interview often starts there. General topics include physical, emotional, cognitive, and social developmental progress (with emphasis on social relations), social environment, family resources and dynamics, critical events, coping history, formal systems involvement, daily living patterns, and other key themes that are salient in this particular person's social history. Typically the interview will gather some information on at least three generations, particularly with regard to any unusual problems, such as genetic disorders, psychiatric problems, or criminal history or about remarkable patterns, such as college graduation or success in business.

One of the most useful tools that a professional has for getting started on a history is the genogram, or family tree. People seem comfortable, even excited, about plotting their family trees. McGoldrick, Gerson, and Shellenberger (1999) have produced an excellent guide and software for mapping a family tree. Making a genogram early in the interview provides a visual reference for the professional and interviewee as they discuss various members of the family and key events. The genogram identifies people in the family system, the nature of their relationship to one another, certain traits, and dates of births, deaths, marriages, and divorces. Details can be added as the story is told, such as identification of various people in the family tree who have an alcohol abuse problem. The entire social history interview can be conducted around a genogram. Examples of genograms are offered in the toolbox in Chapter 6.

Sometimes the social history will focus on a particular topic, such as employability. The interview would focus on history of work, starting in school, after-school activities, and after entering the paid workforce. The professional will still need to gather certain key information, such as structure and dynamics of the family of origin with a focus on what the person learned about work from parents, extended family, social networks, and community influences. DeMaria, Weeks, and Hof (1999) provide useful examples of genograms that focus on particular themes such as attachment, emotions, and culture. Walton and Smith (1999) describe how genograms help with child welfare assessments.

The professional must avoid using a questionnaire as an interrogation tool. The tone should be informal and conversational. Starting with open-ended questions helps the interviewee choose the initial focus and be in control of the flow of information. As the interview proceeds, the interviewer can probe for deeper explanations or more sensitive topics with more specific questions.

The topics in the interview will tend to focus on key life events, including those given prominence by the interviewee as well as significant events in the history of the broader environment. Most life histories emphasize times when major changes occurred or the person had to make a significant decision. In gathering information about life events, the professional should take care to ask about conditions prior to the event, during the event, and after the event, with focus on how the person responded. For example, if a mother is discussing the birth of her first child, the interview will cover how she became pregnant, her anticipation, prenatal condition, the birthing process, her and her baby's condition at birth, and how she adapted to being a mother to this particular child. The professional would also ask about context, such as who was supporting her, where she lived, health care, other concurrent major life events, and other relevant topics.

Some social histories must be rapid and focused, particularly in such contexts as making a kinship care placement recommendation for child protection or determining discharge planning for a patient treated in an emergency room for mental health needs. Abbreviated histories are generally based on topics that are most relevant to the question at hand. The list of topics in Chapter 6 is so broad that the professional should make a quick review to select those that are most critical. If subsequent plans are needed, a deeper history can be conducted.

The professional is most likely to ask closed or direct questions near the end of the interview, when going over the checklist to capture information about overlooked topics. The interview should end at a pre-arranged time, if possible. If more information is needed, then another session should be scheduled. If the person is engrossed in a topic and wants to continue, then, if possible, the professional should continue. The professional should stop asking questions 5 or 10 minutes before the end of the allotted time and review with the interviewee what they have done so far and encourage him or her to ask questions or comment on the process.

Interview Record. The interviewer makes a record as the conversation proceeds, which may involve copious note taking or recording with audio or video equipment. In addition to a direct record of the information provided by the interviewee, professionals constantly make memos about their own reflections. These may include thoughts about themes that are emerging, prompts for questions that should be asked later, observations of emotions that the interviewee expresses while telling the story, or any number of other matters that are not a direct part of the communication at the moment but are on the mind of the professional. When professionals have information from other sources, they might note what is left unsaid.

The professional is likely to make a written summary record of the interview. Some notes will be recorded onto forms about the social history either during the interview or immediately after. This is particularly the case in agencies that have specific required forms for the case record. Other professionals will write a narrative report. In all cases, the record should reflect who was interviewed, the location, date, and start and end times.

The professional will blend information from the multiple interviews with information from other sources (e.g., records and direct observation) to write the descriptive section of the social history report, discussed below.

Records

People who are providing information for a social history may offer a variety of documents and materials about the history. These could include letters, photographs, scrapbooks, journals, newspaper articles, official records, and other sources of information that constitute a record of something about the person's life. Most of the older records are on paper; more recent records may include computer files.

Clients may ask the professional to review certain records. If the client has a copy of his ex-wife's farewell letter or son's high school poems, it may be helpful for the professional to read it as the history is explored. Or going over the old newspaper coverage of a former athletic star's success may help the professional and client discuss the evolution of her midlife depression. Seeing a client's artwork or poetry at various stages of life can be enlightening.

Official records are those maintained at places where the person received service or the government keeps records. For example, the vital statistics unit at the public health department will have birth and death certificates and the Social Security Administration will have formal income records. People accumulate records as they go through school or receive medical services, mental health or addictions treatment, social services (e.g., child welfare, elder protection, and economic assistance programs), or other services. Employers and the military maintain records. If a person has been through civil court, such as for divorce, child support, or bankruptcy, a record exists. If the person has violated a criminal law or been a victim, there will be a record at the law enforcement jurisdictional office and the court. People have credit and banking records. In developed countries, which tend to have elaborate recording and archival capacities, huge amounts of records are amassed about every individual. Some people have copies of many records about themselves and can share them with the professional doing the interview. In some cases, particularly where critical life decisions are at stake, such as adoption or criminal sentencing, it may be necessary to gather documents. Typically, organizational records are the property of the organization. The organizational policies usually allow for release of copies of the records to the person who is the subject of the record but only with the person's explicit written permission and payment of a fee for the cost of copying and sending the record.

In certain cases, such as an adoptee's quest for birth parents (Drake & Sherrill, 2004), a former foster child's search for siblings, or a criminal investigation, the probe of records may require extensive investigation. Skilled investigators can help search for people or records, as can Internet information and books about the process of searching for records or ancestors (King, 1999; Starnes, 2002).

Official records are an excellent way to verify dates, locations, and particular conditions. The tools in Chapter 6 includes the "Checklist for Social History Record Compilation," a guide to potential sources of archived information, as well as a list of potential Web-based and archival sources for locating records.

Direct Observation

The professional creating a social history will also rely on direct observation of the individual, interviewees, and broader environment.

During interviews, unobtrusive observation of the person's appearance and demeanor while the person talks about the social history can stimulate valuable insight into the person's feelings about events in the history and current social functioning. Factors to consider include those listed here, although each person is unique and will present in ways such that the specific list of any one individual will differ from another (Groth-Marnat, 1997):

- *Appearance:* What does the person's appearance say about self-care (e.g., hygiene, grooming), health or mental health (e.g., energy level), self-presentation (e.g., casual or formal), style (e.g., promotes own ethnicity, blends with the background environment), or other attributes?
- *Behavior:* While communicating, note the person's movement, body language, eye contact, facial expressions, voice tone, and other nonverbal expressions.
- *Attention span:* Note whether the person is able to concentrate and avoid distractions.
- *Perception:* Does the person perceive reality in the way most people around him or her do? Are the images he or she conveys missing facts (e.g., indicators of repression or denial)? Are there physiological barriers to accurate perception (e.g., seeing or hearing impairments)?
- *Memory:* Does the person have more accurate memory about less emotional (e.g., height, residence) than emotional events (e.g.,

abuse, accidents)? How much detail can the person recall? Are there differences in short- and long-term memory?

- *Affect and mood:* Is the mood appropriate for the setting? Any evidence of mood-altering substances? What is the general mood and capacity to express emotions (e.g., flat, depressed, elated)?
- *Judgment:* Does the person indicate healthy and moral decision making, such as understanding consequences for behavioral choices?
- *Speech:* Note the person's ability to communicate orally, including any speech impediments, pace of expression, language, extent of vocabulary, cultural context, and tone in terms of confidence, loudness. Is the flow of information coherent or rambling? Spontaneous?
- *Orientation in time and place:* This is an indicator of mental status; for example, does the person know where he or she is, what day it is, and what time? Any indications of drowsiness or confusion?
- *Indications of delusions, hallucinations, or suicidal ideation:* These are signs of serious mental disturbance and warrant referral for further assessment if none has yet been done.

How people present themselves and interact with interviewers is a helpful indicator of how they handle social relations. The presentation of self will vary as the topics of conversation vary. The interviewer should note any changes as they occur.

Of course, the presentation of self will also be affected by the context in which the interview occurs. People will generally be more restrained in a professional's office than in their own home. For that reason, conducting interviews in a home setting is highly desirable, particularly because social histories are so powerfully affected by family dynamics. Understanding the history can be enhanced by observing the physical environment in which the person lives, though it may be considerably different from the environments in which he or she formerly lived as the history evolved.

Observations in the home include attending to such broad categories as:

- Physical environment:
  - What is the décor? Has the family tried to make it attractive and comfortable? Signs of cultural awareness? Note general appearance, for example, furnishings, decorations, expressions of self and family.

- o Does the residence have basic facilities, for example, functional plumbing, refrigeration, heating, cooling, electricity, locks for security?
- o Any structural impairments, for example, roof leaks, floor problems, broken windows, barriers for family members with disabilities, safety hazards?
- o If the house has problems, how does the family cope? For example, tries to fix problem with resources available; avoids it.
- o Note degree of cleanliness and organization in the home.
- o Note signs of pets and their care.

- • Social environment:
  - o Who lives in the home?
  - o Note how the residents interact with one another, for example, frequency and tone of their conversations.
  - o How is personal space organized for individual residents? Balance of personal and collective?
  - o Note indicators of power relations in the home. Does the space indicate accommodations for various member of the family by age, gender, disability, other status?

Particular interviews may require specific focus on other factors, as well. The professional should take care to differentiate that which is situational and that which is chronic. For example, some interviewees will simply have a bad day—they may have a cold, be dealing with a distraction such as need for car repair, or be tired from a long night at work. Their demeanor may reflect a temporary status, not a persistent concern.

The professional should record notes on observations and how they contribute to interpretation of the social history, which happens as the discovery of information proceeds. This step is easy to overlook because the tangible sights, smells, and sounds of the home environment stay vivid in the short-term memory, but they may erode as time goes by. As the professional proceeds to focus on the overall interpretation, details of the observations may be lost unless careful notes are taken.

Information About Community Context

Any solid history review will include a good description and interpretation of the communities in which the person was raised (Garbarino,

1997; Sampson 2000). While the strongest influences on the individual are in the family and home environments, individual development is also affected by factors in the neighborhood and broader geographic area. The number of variables that characterize communities is extensive (Andrews, 1997; Earls & Buka, 2000). Common descriptors include economic conditions, violence rates, quality of schools, employment patterns, housing quality, pollution, police–community relations, disasters, political system, transportation, and social cohesion. Direct observation of the communities can be revealing, as the professional sees firsthand such situations as finely landscaped or unkempt yards, children playing in the streets or on safe playgrounds, signs of drinking or of volunteer fundraising at street corners, and other indicators of community life.

Records can provide contextual information. For example, a media exposé about substandard conditions at a children's orphanage where the client lived can verify the client's recollections of neglect. Statistical reports at the neighborhood or community level can describe the housing, poverty, crime, public health threats, school performance, hazards in the physical environment, and other factors that affect the lives of residents. Geographically based data can now be found in multiple sources. They include U.S. Census data, newspaper accounts, reports of regional planning commissions, planning and study documents for schools, and area plans for such topics as economic development, health and human services agencies, housing, and environmental protection. Public data are typically geocoded and can be accessed by Internet; they provide small area descriptions using Geographic Information Systems (GIS). Chapter 6 contains additional information about community assessment.

Referrals for Focused Assessments

In clinical cases, identification of certain themes may indicate the need for a specialized evaluation of an individual, such as assessment of mental retardation, genetic markers, psychological functioning, or neurological examination. In many cases these assessments have already been conducted or there is a record of such assessments throughout the life history. These assessments are generally based on use of standardized psychological, educational, or medical protocols and instruments administered by skilled professionals. They may involve a multidisciplinary evaluation with contributions from a team of specialists. Each of these assessments produces a report and is communicated to the person who is the focus of the report and the person's family. The social history should include a summary of the findings from the assessments and, significantly, information about how the person and family responded to the results of the assessment. If an assessment detected a problem, the history will reflect how the client and other family members felt about the finding and whether the assessment led to effective intervention to address the problem.

Sometimes the assessment will focus on the family as a system. Several hundred, perhaps more than a thousand, standardized instruments have been developed to assess family system functioning. Snyder, Cavell, Heffer, and Mangrum (1995) discuss the complexity of assessing family systems because of the multiple levels involved. The assessment might focus on an individual's perspective on his or her family, a dyad (e.g., marital partners or one parent and child), a small subset of the family (e.g., sibling group, two separated parents and a child), the nuclear family, or the extended family network. Snyder and his colleagues list several family assessment techniques appropriate at each level. These instruments generally aim to assess the dynamic functioning and processes within the family.

At times, in addition to or instead of a full interview, a more structured family history assessment may be useful. Chapter 6 of this book includes a synopsis of several commonly used assessment tools that focus on the whole family system for purposes of gathering a history of events.

Data Gathering Pitfalls

Chapter 1 addresses ethical issues for professionals as they search for the truth that lies under social histories and pursue fidelity to the meaning that people make of their histories. This section extends that discussion by reviewing techniques for managing problems that might arise while gathering information for a social history. Typical concerns include trust, power, interviewer bias, memory, and credibility.

Trust. For people who have sensitive and emotionally painful events in their histories, it may take several interviews to establish trust. Until they feel trust, they will withhold critical information or resist the interviews by doing such things as failing to show for appointments. They need time to become familiar with the professional. Experience with the professional's nonjudgmental response to matters under discussion will facilitate trust. The professional delays raising sensitive topics until the person is obviously comfortable and ready to reveal feelings. If the professional does not have extended time, sometimes trust can be enhanced by reaching out to the mistrustful person through a trusted mediator. For example, a mistrustful battered woman may have a trusted friend or advocate from a survivor's program who will sit in the interview with her. Steps should be taken to ensure confidentiality by the third party.

Power. Within the class structure of society, professionals often wield exceptional power relative to the interviewee and his or her family (Reed-Danahay, 2001). Social histories are often performed within service settings where the person has come for some sort of assistance. Many of these interviewees are economically poor, members of minority groups, people with disabilities, children who were rejected, survivors of all sorts of traumatic events and losses, and people affected by drugs or alcohol or by physical or mental illness. They rarely have the educational level of the interviewer. They are accustomed to living in a world where they are marginalized, excluded from and looked down upon by people in the mainstream of society. The power differential is even more severe when the social history is being conducted under involuntary or semi-voluntary conditions, such as in cases of child protection, sentencing mitigation, or addiction treatment.

Many have learned to cope with threats from powerful people by minimizing or denying their emotions, avoiding direct communication, releasing selective information, and otherwise trying to retain a semblance of dignity and personal control. They are often quite congenial while pretending to know or revealing very little.

As with trust building, the professional must exercise patience in managing power differentials. Cultural competence in relating across social class is absolutely essential. Professionals can set the tone for open discussions across class lines by how they dress, such as minimizing jewelry or other luxurious accessories, and how they behave, such as showing comfort in the interviewee's unkempt home. Professionals' understanding of their own power and general self-awareness is the first step toward managing power differences.

Interviewer Bias. Professionals' biases may affect how they focus attention, gather information, and make interpretive observations. Groth-Marnat (1997, p. 73) notes several ways that bias may emerge during an assessment. A "halo" effect happens when interviewers form a general impression and then infer other characteristics, as when they begin to believe that a gregarious, articulate client is more competent at solving problems than a quiet one. A "primacy" effect suggests that first impressions will bias later judgments; for example, if a female client is late for the first appointment, the professional may believe her to be a procrastinating person. Physical attractiveness may cause the interviewer to de-emphasize pathology in a person with serious mental illness. One outstanding characteristic, such as obesity, may cause the professional to believe that other characteristics of the person are related to that one.

Professionals may also show bias when the person's values or behaviors are the same as or different from their own. For example, it may be hard for a professional to maintain a nonjudgmental stance while watching a mother hold a switch from a tree and occasionally threaten to swat a child. There may be no signs of overt child abuse, but use of force, particularly with objects such as belts, violates the professional's values and training about how to discipline children. Conversely, if the person prefers bluegrass music and the professional does, too, then there may be a positive bias toward the person's view of things.

Maintaining objectivity is an art that can be cultivated only with intense self-reflection and continual peer consultation and supervision. Self- and peer review is a life-long professional practice.

Memory. The development of the social history will flounder when informants demonstrate memory problems. How well a person recalls facts will vary by time of day and degree of mental fatigue (Plummer, 2001). The person may have cognitive impairment associated with mental retardation, learning disabilities, sensory disabilities, language barriers, cultural oppression, or psychological conditions. Memory problems can be expected in people who experience trauma in early childhood (Henry, Moffitt, Caspi, Langley, & Silva, 1994; Howe, 2000; Loftus, 1993) because repressing the memories to avoid reliving the pain can be a useful coping mechanism. The professional should take care not to disrupt psychological coping through repression by inducing unwanted floods of emotions as memories are recalled, unless the client is in therapy with the professional and ready to release feelings and acquire news ways of coping. If the professional is primarily trying to help complete a social history assessment, one of the best ways to deal with memory problems is, with the person's permission, to talk with collateral sources—people who know the person's history and are able to remember the facts and details. For example, sometimes a sibling is the best informant about a brother's abuse history, or a grandparent can relate how a grandchild experienced her parent's death.

Credibility or Reliability of the Information. If, as the history emerges, the professional detects significant inconsistencies or false information, problems with credibility and reliability will arise. Tips for assessing credibility were discussed in Chapter 1.

With regard to inconsistencies, the professional should work through the various versions of the information to ascertain which is most accurate. For example, if a man referred to having finished high school and a sibling said he never graduated, checking the facts may indicate that the man was referring to having completed a GED while the sibling was referring to his not having completed the full diploma.

Informants may offer vague or misinformation because they are unfamiliar with events in the history or unsure of how to describe them. This particularly occurs when reporting histories of mental illness. They may be unable to adequately describe a condition, saying, for example, "She had spells." The professional should get as detailed a behavioral description about the "spells" as possible to determine what sort of symptoms may have occurred. The professional should be familiar with or search out the meaning of culturally used terms. For example, rural southerners use the term *sugar*, as in "she had sugar," to refer to diabetes.

In rare cases, informants will blatantly lie to the professional. Sometimes they are disturbed and relating delusional information that they themselves believe. Other times they are aiming to deceive the person for reasons of social desirability or self-aggrandizement. For example, I interviewed a man in prison after he was convicted of several sex offenses. He stated that he was in prison due to his drinking and violence and specifically denied ever having made a sexual assault. In cases of deception that are detected by the professional, the *events* of the social history should be written without reliance on false information that was provided by the person aiming to distort the truth, although the person's telling a *narrative* that includes false statements should be included as an event in itself.

Effective Data Gathering. Through interviews, records review, and direct observation, professionals can capture the essence of a social history if they follow a few basic principles of effective communication and professional practice (Heyl, 2001). They should listen and observe actively, respectfully, and nonjudgmentally, while maintaining accurate and confidential records of the data collected. Each professional should spend time alone and with peers sharpening his self-awareness and cultural competence. All information that is gathered should be assessed with attention to the context from which it emerged, including the interactive processes among people in the context as well as broader social and historical forces that affected the life events.

Organizing and Writing the Social History Description

When a professional prepares a written or oral report, the first of two major parts will be the social history description. The second, the interpretation, is discussed in the next chapter.

The social history description typically follows the outline listed below. The narrative chronology that forms the core of the report is written by the professional and reviewed by the person who is the topic of the assessment. The narrative is often supplemented by figures and attachments such as those discussed below.

Social History Report: Part One—Description of the History

Cover Page. The report begins with a cover page that contains information such as:

- If relevant, name of agency or auspices under which the history is conducted
- Client's full name
- Client's date of birth
  - o Prepared by: Information about who prepared the report: Name, degree, licensure, address
- Date of the start of the social history assessment
- Date of the report
- Purpose of the report
  - o For example, "Prepared at the request of the client upon hospitalization at [name of hospital] on [date] for treatment related to intoxication by alcohol"
- List of contents
  - o This lists all parts of the report, which typically include cover page, list of sources, chronology, opinion and recommendations (the interpretation discussed in the next chapter), and attached figures such as genogram, sociogram, time line, and/or map
- List of sources
  - o All sources upon which the preparer relied; the list is organized by type of source—typically one section for interviews and one for records; detailed information about the sources, including names and dates, should be included

For example, here is an excerpt (not the complete list) from a source list for a social history report:

⌒ Interviews ⌒

Brad Gepford	Subject	5/29/06 (1.5 hrs); 6/6/06 (1.5 hrs); 7/2/06 (1 hr)
Mildred Simmons	Grandmother	6/25/06 (1.5 hrs)
Ted Gepford	Father	6/16/06 (1.5 hrs)
Anna Gepford	Mother	6/4/06 (2.25 hr)
Sofia Gepford	Sister	6/6/06 by phone (.5 hr)
Mary Tare	Paternal aunt	6/16/06 (1 hr)
Sue Ingles	Cousin	6/13/06 (1 hr)
Luanne Moran	Former stepmother	7/25/06 (1 hr)
Thelma Daly	Former stepmother	8/6/06 (.45 hr)

⌒ Records ⌒

Golden County DSS [case of Brad Gepford]

    Intake, Face Sheet, Determination of Fact Sheet (7/31/04)

    Case evaluation summary 10/7/04

    Action log report, 6pp 10/8/04

    Investigative matrix report, 5pp 10/8/04

    2nd investigative matrix report, 4pp 10/8/04

    Case staffing notes, 2pp, 10/7/04

    Releases by Anna Gepford, 3pp, 8/2/04

    Intake Summary Report, Anna Gepford 5pp [no date]

Employment of Brad Gepford

    3/12/01–5/26/06, Winn Dixie employment records

    6/16/04–8/16/04, Urban League summer program

Health records of Brad Gepford

    Golden Medical Center ER visit, 7/30/04

    Golden Medical Center ER visit, 5/27/06

Mental health evaluations of Brad Gepford

    6/17/06 Neuropsychological evaluation by Celia Jones, PhD
    6/22/06 Psychiatric evaluation by Antonio Lòpez, MD

Often the source list is included as an attachment, though sometimes it precedes the chronology because sources of facts are listed on the chronology and the reader will have an overview of what the various sources were.

Chronology. Life histories are best understood when they are presented in chronological order so that the sequence of key events as the subject experienced them and the proximity of various events to one another are clearly shown. Professionals include only those facts that they believe are reliable—that is, reflect the truth of the story and have fidelity to the meaning that people in the story give to the events. The statements in a chronology relay what happened and people's impressions about the events. The impressions are derived from interviews, assessments by evaluators (such as educators or mental health professionals who made records of the events), and other record keepers (such as people who made notes in journals or medical records).

The professional begins writing the chronology as the history taking begins. The chronology is a working document on which to record dates, main events, sources, and notes for her further research into the history. The format is as follows:

Sample Working Chronology

Date	Event	Source	Notes
5/27/06	Brad enters GMC ER with gunshot wound	GMC Medical Records	Talk to ER MD or nurse
5/27/06	Anna is treated for "panic attack" while with Brad at the ER; she fears losing Brad the way she lost her father	Interview with AG 6/4/06	Check for Hx of any MH problems re: Anna

The chronology emerges from the professional's notes and memos written during the interviews. Rarely will the interview information be in chronological order. The professional constructs a draft chronology based on the interview notes and then makes additional notes directly on the chronology while reviewing other records or conducting further interviews. While the chronology is in draft form, information that has questionable reliability may be included.

When all the information is gathered and the professional has determined the credibility and reliability of the various sources, the professional removes that which is unreliable and prepares the final chronology, which is much like the table above, without the "Notes" column. An extended excerpt from a finished chronology is presented with the tools in Chapter 6.

Attachments. The social history often includes figures, discussed in Chapter 5, that help to illustrate the major themes in the history. The chronology and these figures extract critical points from a complex, massive amount of information as a basis for the most important part of the social history assessment, the interpretation, discussed in Chapter 5.

The figures are discussed in detail in Chapter 6. The attachments almost always include a genogram. Sometimes the relationships among a subset of people on the genogram are further explained by a sociogram (also known as an ecomap) that depicts the dynamics of these relationships.

The chronology may be crystallized into a life history calendar or an even shorter time line of major events. This is particularly useful when a multidisciplinary team is going to review the case and the narrative chronology is quite long. Judges also prefer a time line in forensic cases. Producing these figures helps the professional to analyze the case and synthesize the core themes before forming an opinion about the history.

Conclusion: Describing the History

Unfortunately, in many settings the social history assessment stops here. In some settings personnel are unprepared to do the full assessment. Funding restrictions cause some organizations to put minimally qualified personnel in positions that involve gathering information to describe a life, leaving out the critical focus on interpreting the life, which requires considerable professional knowledge about theory and human behavior. In other settings the significance of the social environment as a contributor to individual development and well-being is minimized, with emphasis placed on individual behavior and efficacy.

The life story has value in itself, just as a portrait or snapshot can communicate rich information about a person. The full value of the history, though, is best realized when it serves as a foundation for the formation of an opinion and recommendations. Carefully gathering comprehensive, relevant, and reliable information and then summarizing it into narrative and visual descriptions is essentially a means to the end of deriving meaning from the history. The opinion based on these descriptions can then address the core purpose for which the assessment is being made.

5

Making Meaning
Interpreting the Social History

So what does the social history *mean?* Together, the professional and client, who may be an individual or social system such as a family, will interpret the history. The interpretation is grounded in reflection, the careful and thoughtful contemplation of the facts in the history. In dialogue, the subject brings his or her ideas and emotions concerning what certain experiences meant when they happened and what they mean now. The professional brings ideas grounded in careful processes of analysis and synthesis of the descriptive themes in the history. Together, the professional and client can develop meaning relative to the purpose of the assessment, which may be for personal insight and development, therapy, documenting a family history, making recommendations to a court or other authority, or other reasons.

The social history assessment reveals dominant patterns of social strengths, that is, the person's social behaviors that are adaptive and promote well-being, and vulnerabilities, which are the tendencies to stagnate or induce harm (Kaplan & Girard, 1994; Kuchl, 1995). The history can suggest the future conditions under which the person is likely to function well or comfortably and those under which there will be strain or dysfunction. Thus the history assessment can inform transformative action for positive change when needed.

This chapter summarizes essential approaches to interpreting a history and demonstrates the process and product through a detailed case example.

The theory and knowledge covered in Chapters 2 and 3 form an essential foundation for guiding interpretation that is based on a professional perspective.

The Process of Developing the Professional Opinion

The interpretation occurs as the story emerges. The process is both deductive, applying established theories that fit the facts, and inductive, revealing unique theories based on the facts. As professionals gather information through interviews and other sources, they begin work on a "case theory" by maintaining reflective notes about alternative interpretive themes (Bisman, 1999). They test these alternatives by asking questions and sharing ideas with the person. Their ideas are grounded in the unique facts of the person's life and their knowledge of theory about human behavior in the social environment, reviewed in Chapters 2 and 3. As professionals explore possible themes in the life history, they may consult literature about research and theory on specialized topics. For example, when a client talked about his brother's autism, I reviewed professional information on autism and its potential effects on family systems.

The professional should take care to avoid using a fixed approach to every case, such as always focusing on attachment or power dynamics in relationships. The constellation of salient themes in each person's life is beautifully unique, so the testing and application of theory relative to the case should be significantly informed by the facts of the life story. Professional practice involves protecting the perspective and voice of the person who is the subject of the history so that the professional's lens does not dominate the interpretation. For example, if a professional believes a child who experienced sexual molestation is likely to have been traumatized, but the client communicates the experience in a way that suggests regret and sadness over betrayal but not trauma, then the professional should avoid imposing his or her own assumptions onto the interpretation of the situation.

The history will be long and complex, requiring close communication between the professional and the client to determine what is most significant. As the story unfolds, asking clients what certain events meant to them at the time they occurred will help create a record of significant events. When the descriptive portion of the social history is complete, a helpful exercise involves having the person review the facts and reflect on that which mattered most. Professionals can also point to events that seemed to exert significant influence, using their objective lens to encourage the client's fresh perspectives. The professional is also in a position to make observations about the unusual absence of typical events that might go unnoticed by the subject of the history. People are generally unaware of what they may have missed. For example, in the United States, only a few adults experience childhoods with freedom from ever having lost a parent or loved one to death, divorce, or abandonment. They often fail to realize how fortunate they are. People may also be unaware of misfortune that the professional will observe, such as exceptionally weak affection or neglect from family and social networks.

The professional integrates information from multiple sources as a basis for the analysis, including observations of the person's social behavior as exhibited in the interviews with the professional or in other social settings, content of the interviews and records, the person's style of communicating her life history and expressing meaning about it, and knowledge of context such as culture and historical time.

In addition to identifying significant events and their meaning, which involves focusing on parts of the history, the interpretation involves expressing the wholeness of the history through overarching themes. No magic formula exists to guide the discovery of themes. Many disciplines have developed methods to guide analysis of qualitative data such as that found in a life history, particularly for psychosocial purposes (Atkinson, 1998; Bedrosian & Bozicas, 1994; Strauss & Corbin, 1998). Ultimately, the professional art of clinical judgment and mature analysis and synthesis of data about human behavior, grounded in supervised practice and experience, forms the basis for the opinion.

Though the specific methods may vary, the interpretation of the history evolves from an analysis process that extracts themes from the information. Generally this analysis involves listing as many categorical ideas as can be identified in the total history (coding). The professional compares the various codes to one another; weighs them in terms of frequency, intensity, or other indicator of salience; and then clusters them into themes, thus reducing the amount of information to be considered. By creating themes, the professional is forming a basis for a theory of the case, which can be tested by asking the client relevant questions regarding the relative validity of each theme or weaving questions into the continual interviewing process with various informants. The next step is to look for patterns among the themes.

The analytic process reduces the data to core themes and patterns, thus losing some of the richness of the initial details of the life story. The professional then synthesizes the information, blending the themes and patterns with knowledge from theory and practice into an interpreted synopsis of the history with illustrations, often quotations, drawn from the original data.

Discovering Interpretive Themes

Capturing the essential themes in an entire life history can be a daunting endeavor. The human service professional will look for particular patterns in the information, including, but not limited to, repetitions, systems dynamics, social relations, transitions, and ecological context.

Repetitions

Certain event characteristics tend to repeat themselves over time within one life or social system or over generations in a family system. Many factors are known to repeat across generations, such as artistic productivity, perpetration of family violence, crime victimization, school success, political leadership, extramarital relations, athletic competence, schizophrenia, and many more.

For example, alcohol abuse is notoriously repetitious, cropping up like fruit across family trees. Family members will rarely say, "Uncle Ted was an alcoholic." They might say, "Uncle Ted . . . had a drinking problem," " . . . couldn't hold his liquor," or " . . . liked to party." When prompted with skilled questions, the narrator might reveal that Uncle Ted drank every Saturday night to the point of no control or passing out and that he had problems with job stability because his hangovers often lasted until Monday, and that people avoided Ted's grandfather because he was so moody due to drinking. Then there was Cousin Sue whom the family rarely saw but when they did, she seemed spacey, and then she checked herself into a rehab center.

Within a life, a person might experience repetitious phenomena. Some people will have anniversary reactions on the date a traumatic event occurred. Some will perpetuate family tendencies to protect certain secrets, such as sexual abuse or gambling. Others must deal with multiple deaths of loved ones or celebrate repeated lucky events such as winning lotteries or reaping benefits of land values that quickly escalate. Some rise to the top wherever they are while others struggle to overcome repeated failure in various settings. Repetitious patterns in relationships, symptoms of problems, ways of functioning, genetic anomalies—such redundancies in a life history are critical indicators of how a person has developed and currently functions.

Systems Dynamics

Each person is a part of multiple social systems at home, school, work, and in the community. The history will reveal much about how the systems function. Is each system static or dynamic? Open or closed? Rigid or flexible? What other traits do the systems have? How does the person navigate among the various systems, particularly if their characteristics are different? For example, how does a child from a permissive household function in an authoritarian school?

Family systems have their own dynamics. When partners marry, form households together, and/or have children, they bring the different dynamics from their backgrounds into the formation of a new system. How this system compares to the systems of origin can contribute considerable meaning to factors in the social history interpretation.

Snyder, Cozzi, and Mangrum (2002, pp. 70–71) propose a conceptual model for assessing couples and families that involves examining five domains at each system level (individuals within the system; dyads such as spouses, siblings, or parent-child; nuclear family; extended family and related social systems; and community and cultural systems). The five domains are those typically assessed in families:

- *Cognition:* What is the capacity for understanding? What are the core beliefs—what do people believe about themselves, the systems of which they are a part, the world, spiritual power? The professional will assess how clients perceive their own self-image and whether that is consistent with the image others have of them. What does the system value? What assumptions and standards does the system have regarding members' behavior? Are there irrational beliefs within the system?
- *Affect:* What are the dominant expressed emotions in the system? What is the general mood? Factors such as cohesion, expressiveness, satisfaction, commitment, and tolerance might appear in this assessment. At the community levels, feelings of belonging or alienation would be noted.
- *Communication and interpersonal relations:* How do people in the system process information? How do people relate harmoniously and how do they handle conflict? To what extent does the system seek and receive social support? How do people mobilize essential resources?
- *Structural and developmental components:* How do individuals manage themselves across various systems? What are the main

sources of stress? How do people cope? Given that various individuals within the systems are at different points in the life course, how do developmental issues affect their relationships? What is the hierarchy within the system?

- *Control, sanctions, and related behaviors:* How is power distributed in the system? How do individuals regulate their own behavior and influence the behavior of others? How are decisions made? Does anxiety lead the person to seek ways to manipulate the social environment for safety or control?

The family system will be the dominant system in most people's lives, but other social networks operate as systems, too, and the person's experiences within those systems will also shed light on the history interpretation.

Social Relations and Resources

The history will reveal how a person behaves socially with other people and across social settings over time. These three foci—interactions, settings, and time—indicate consistencies and variability in the person's social behavior and experiences. Further, personal lives vary with regard to the amount and quality of social resources they have, which also vary over time.

The focus on interactions will summarize processes of communication, power, emotional expression, and other factors that constitute the social functioning of the individual and various people around him or her. Family systems theory will help to guide interpretation of social relations, guiding observation of such patterns as boundaries, coalitions within systems, and hierarchies.

How have other people influenced the individual and how has the individual influenced other people? Adults who actively interact with children, speaking with them and not to them, listening actively, will promote more open expression in a child than adults who persistently direct children, paying little attention to or punishing the child's expressions. How have these parenting styles affected the individual and persisted over time?

The interactions may be fairly stable across settings or change from one to another—professionals will make notes about this as they review the history. Nurturing adults typically teach children how to behave across settings, for example, to be active on a playground and calm while visiting a hospital. People tend to be more comfortable in some settings than others. They may say, "I just don't feel like myself when I'm there." Some people have social anxiety and withdraw from as many social settings as possible, staying as close to home as they can. Certain settings will create or hinder opportunities for social expression. For example, services at houses of worship vary from one culture to another. Some encourage standing, dancing, or speaking back to the leader of the service. Others insist on absolute reserve in behavior except when directed by the leader. A highly active person will have difficulty sitting still for long periods at the latter service.

The professional will look for patterns of social relations and particularly observe any signs of incongruent behavior. For example, a common concern is the person who discloses private family matters to numerous colleagues at work. The social environment of most work settings is that most employees will focus only superficially on personal topics and save personal matters for conversations with close friends or family.

To illustrate patterns of interaction across settings and time, consider the young man who behaves quietly in a family system where people avoid conflict and agitation. He may be the most aggressive player on the basketball court, releasing emotions as well as physical energy in the context of organized team sport. His behavior varies across settings. Over time, as older people within the family pass away and younger people bring new friends and mates into the system, the reticence at home may change and expression become more open.

The focus on social resources will attend to matters of social support and conflict. As noted in Chapter 3, social support includes instrumental assistance, such as making transportation or money available, and emotional support like affirmation, encouragement, and comfort. A person may receive ample instrumental support but little emotional care, as when a parent begrudgingly pays child support to a noncustodial child. Or emotional support may be plenty while instrumental resources are withheld, as in the case of a family trying to help an addict recover, or unavailable, as in cases of poverty. Support often comes with ambivalent messages, as when a mother does whatever she can for her young adult daughter who is a single parent but she persistently doles out criticism with the support. Also, social resources are simply not equitably distributed in the world. Some people are born with multiple caregivers who shower affection and guidance on the child. Others barely have one stable caregiver or none at all and are shifted from one partially attached caregiver to another.

How people receive social support will affect how they learn to give support. The professional will observe patterns of giving and receiving support while interpreting the history.

Transitions and Their Impact

Lives are marked by normative transitions, such as birth of a sibling, finishing school, marrying, death of an elderly grandparent, and retirement, to name only a few. Lives are also affected by critical events that precipitate transitions, such as the unexpected death of a parent, relocation to another community or nation, victimization, accidents, or promotion to a position of leadership. Each transition—whether marked by predominantly positive or negative emotions—requires adaptation. People adapt in many diverse and unique ways.

The descriptive part of a social history records all the major transitions. The interpretive part will focus on how the individual responded to the transition and how it affected social functioning over time. For example, when talking about a critical life event in a woman's social history, collateral informants may say, "She was never the same after that happened." That opens the opportunity for a dialogue about just how she changed. The changes often precipitate new transitions, as when a divorce leads to a job change and subsequent relocation. And so the life evolves.

How people handle life transitions reveals their major areas of competence. What are the dominant patterns of social strengths—that is, social behaviors that are adaptive and promote well-being—and vulnerabilities, those tendencies that cause stagnation or that induce harm? People will often focus on their problems and overlook their assets. Formerly, health and human services professionals tended to do likewise, emphasizing deficits. In recent decades training has recognized that the key to building social competence is strengthening assets, so professionals will help the person and others concerned with the person's future to recognize and enhance assets. Close qualitative examination of how transitions affected the life and how the individual coped will be a key to understanding the individual's social functioning.

Ecological Context

How have forces in the broader environment affected the individual? People are personally affected by such events as loss of health insurance (the government provides no universal coverage), a family member's job loss (the local office closed because the company moved its operations offshore), media messages that a particular weight loss program or drug prescription will make them feel better, and a military friend's deployment to war. Each life is lived in specific places, at certain historical times, and in political contexts.

The interpretation will involve a close look at how the person and the people in the person's social networks responded to the ecological forces. For example, if a family member lost a job when the company moved the work to China, did the various family members attribute the loss to fate, political decisions that undermine the U.S. and global economies, the ineptness of the person who lost the job, tough luck in a country that needs to provide more support to other nations, God's will, or other reasons? Do they see the loss as an opportunity for change or grounds for withdrawal and despair? Do they feel active, passive, or neutral about what happened locally?

The main issue is not just what happened but how the person and social system coped with the effects of the ecological forces. An ecological chart or discussion (see Chapter 6) can facilitate presentation of such an interpretation.

Weaving Themes

No history assessment can address every possible theme presented in Chapters 2 and 3 or mentioned here, and there are many, many others. The art of synthesizing a social history is to identify those themes that seem to have the most influence on the life—those that became predominant and exerted the most significant influence over the life. Many people will focus on certain areas of their social functioning—for example, relations with intimate partners, parents, or workplace colleagues. The person's preferences and concerns will help shape the foci of the interpretive themes.

As the themes are identified, the professional will work with the person to weave the themes together into a cohesive summary that helps the person perceive fresh meaning in the social history. It may be helpful to draw a visual figure to illustrate the conceptual ideas that summarize the themes (see Chapter 6).

The Professional Opinion. When social history assessments are conducted by professionals in conjunction with the subject of the history as part of a therapeutic relationship, the professional and client work together to interpret the history. The meaning that the client and the professional perceive in the history may differ because they each see the life through their own lenses. They then share their perspectives.

Social history assessments are also often done by professionals for the purpose of rendering a professional opinion. The opinion may be sought by a judge who has to make a decision in a case (e.g., adoption or criminal sentencing), a multidisciplinary team (e.g., treatment planning for managing a disability or mental illness), a guardian (e.g., the subject has been found to be incompetent to make decisions for him- or herself), or for other reasons. In some cases, the person is an involuntary participant in the process, as in cases of child protection. In cases that require a professional opinion, the person's perspectives are taken into account by the professional, but the focus is on the meaning the professional has attributed to the history.

Finishing the Assessment Report. Chapter 4 reviewed all sections of the assessment report except the last. The social history interpretation ends with a summary report that synthesizes the various themes.

Sometimes the report extends to include recommendations for future action based on the interpretation, although the social history is often a part of a broader assessment that includes biological, psychological, educational, vocational, or other assessments. The history assessment is one part of the information that forms a foundation for recommendations for future action.

The product of the interpretive process is best explained through case examples. Two follow.

Case Examples[1]

No two social history assessments are alike. Each life is unique in facts, patterns, and themes. The inductive process of discovering theory to express meaning about the life experiences yields different social portraits each time and thus the product is somewhat different in each case.

Due to space limitations, the examples offered here are excerpts from full reports. Interpretive social history assessments can fill volumes. To be useful, they must also be presented in summary form. The examples here illustrate how that can be done, with the acknowledgment that each professional will find innovative ways to portray history assessments.

Case 1: Example of Descriptive and Interpretive Themes: Excerpt From Professional Notes for Oral Report to Forensic Multidisciplinary Team

The first case was chosen to illustrate the major categories of themes as they are presented in this book. This is by no means the only way to organize a case interpretation, but seemed to be appropriate in this case. The notes were made by a social worker on a forensic team assigned to determine Damon's mental competency to stand trial. This excerpt does not lead to a conclusion about competence. It essentially summarizes one source of evidence, the social history, which is a part of a comprehensive assessment conducted by a team that included a social worker, psychologist, psychiatrist, addictions specialist, and educational specialist (regarding learning disability). The format here is an outline because the social worker prepared these notes for an oral presentation to the team.

Case synopsis: Social history of a married man (Damon), age 20, who killed his wife during a fit of rage while withdrawing from methamphetamines. Damon was abandoned in infancy by his mother and raised by his alcoholic father. He married his high school sweetheart, Tawanna, two days after they both finished vocational high school. They lived next door to her parents, both alcoholics who never fully accepted Damon. Damon worked steadily under his uncle's supervision at his car service center and Tawanna worked sporadically but could not keep a job. In the months before the assault, Tawanna was spending more time at her parents' and friends' homes than in the trailer with Damon. Damon lost his job when his uncle's business could no longer compete with the franchised service centers. Damon found a new job but hated it. He started increasing his use of drugs to ease the anxiety he was experiencing. One weekend he and Tawanna had a vicious argument that was precipitated by his wanting to have sex and make a baby. Tawanna said she didn't want children. It lasted for hours. They had no drugs at hand and were highly irritable. Damon recalls part of the assault but his memory becomes clear only at the time he was sitting in the living room and the police arrived (called by the neighbors). He expresses intense grief over losing Tawanna.

Descriptive themes are those based on factual evidence. Interpretive themes are those based on the social assessment (interviews with Damon (D) and social network members and records review).

Theme 1: Social stability

1a. Descriptive themes:

- Lived in same house with his father (single parent) consistently through upbringing (except for two periods of less than a week each in foster care)
- Consistent demonstration of affection from and frequent contact with aunt and her family
- Aunt and other extended family households show high regard for children

- D regarded by coworkers and family as pleasant, "sweet" disposition
- D interested in and starting on a career path in auto repair
- No recorded behavioral problems at school or work
- D made a commitment by marrying his girlfriend

1b. Interpretive themes—effect on D's social functioning:

- D expressed and demonstrated strong values about commitment to family stability
- D conforms to social expectations, including requirement of the law and organizations (e.g., school and work); except for undetected drug use, he has no history of criminal offenses
- D has good skills for social interaction though he is shy and withdrawn in novel situations
- D demonstrates competence in work performance
- D is somewhat dependent on the predictability of the social environment—changes generate anxiety

Theme 2: Maltreatment

2a. Descriptive themes:

- Mother left him at age six months (she left him and his father to escape father's domestic violence against her)
- Physical abuse by dad against D (DSS founded case: bruises, broken foot)
- Sexual abuse by dad against D (DSS founded case: coerced sexual relations with dad's girlfriend)
- Neglect by dad of D (DSS founded case: lack of supervision)
- Psychological abuse: (D and others report the following)
  o Perceived abandonment by mom
  o Dad "constantly" told D he was worthless, unwanted
  o Terror by dad (after dad caused D to have a broken foot when he shoved him, D feared death when dad made threats)
  o Exposure to domestic violence by dad against his partners
  o Exposure to dad's alcohol and drug abuse
  o Inconsistencies, especially differences in aunt's and dad's households
  o Lack of available social support—family always supported dad, denied his behavior was inappropriate
  o Lack of effective formal supports—for example, when DSS or law enforcement tried to change his father's behavior, both were ineffective—dad essentially continued harmful behavior, regardless of intervention—state was powerless relative to dad

2b. Interpretive themes—effects of maltreatment on D:

- D fears rejection and yearns to please dad, aunt, and others, therefore is regarded as pleasant
- Repressed fear and anger at dad
- Wishful thinking re: ideal home, yearning for mother
- Numb, "low key" expression of emotions; avoidance of conflict
- Withdrawal, social isolation
- Insecure attachments to marital partner, dad, extended family
- Feelings of inadequacy, believes he can't do anything right, can't handle life's problems, can't even do job right without drugs
- Dependency on wife, other family members
- Inadequate skill in handling frustration; passivity in the face of life's problems (e.g., failure to seek help because of belief that no one can or will help)
- After initial exposure to drugs, desire for drugs to enhance feelings of competence, regular use on the job, inability to handle the anxiety of withdrawal from drugs on weekends

Theme 3: Chaos

3a. Descriptive themes:

- Constantly changing immediate household—father's multiple partners (at least nine different live-in partners during D's childhood)
- Father's unpredictable behavior and lack of consistency in discipline
- Dad's messy household, no daily routine
- Threat of DSS taking him away

3b. Interpretive themes: Effects of chaos on D:

- Uncertainty and anxiety about future; weak sense of personal control and ability to influence consequences
- Mistrusted wife, feared abandonment by wife
- Lack of understanding about how to live in a marital relationship
- Problems in self-discipline

Additional themes apply in this case; only three—one strength (social stability) and two vulnerabilities (maltreatment and chaos)—have been selected for this example. The descriptive themes essentially summarize the facts of the history as they emerged from interviews with Damon, interviews with the aunt, the father, a cousin, and a coworker, and a review of records from the child protection agency and schools. The interpretive themes are added by the professional based on observations of Damon's historical behavior and comments he and others have made about the meaning he attributes to various life events. For example, descriptively, everyone agreed that his father's household was unpredictable and chaotic. The effect this had on Damon, according to the interpretation, is that he became persistently anxious about his relationships with his wife and demonstrated poor social skills in managing his relationship with her.

In the next step, the social worker synthesizes some of the many themes in the case.

Synopsis of social functioning:

This young man values committed relationships and yearns for an idealized, stable household situation. But he demonstrates insufficient capacity to independently handle normal life stresses, such as completing household chores, engaging in and resolving conflict, and feeling competent at his job. He tries too hard to comply with the wishes of others and feels frustrated and anxious about his abilities. He prefers not to express his own desires and instead, withdraws, ignores others, and uses alcohol or drugs to sedate his feelings. His choice of crystal meth promotes a sense of competence while he is using but his profound anxieties are exacerbated when he is withdrawing. His school and work history indicates poor problem-solving capacity except when guided by others. When faced with what he perceives to be extreme social demands, he can respond with sullen anger. He has no history of violent assaults prior to this situation. His history indicates he had affection for and was dependent on his wife.

The synopsis succinctly expresses the social worker's opinion, based on interaction with the client system (Damon and his family), about how the history affected Damon's social functioning. At this point the social history assessment is still essentially descriptive—it describes Damon's current social functioning based on how the history affected the development of his functioning. Again, it will be noted that this is only part of the actual assessment, the part based in the themes chosen for illustration here.

To illustrate what additional information the social worker used in forming an interpretive opinion about these select themes, following is a summary of pertinent theories that influenced the social worker's professional lens.

Theoretical framework:

Traumatic stress and coping: Chronic abuse induced Damon's attempts to minimize aggravating others by being passive, trying to please others, and denying expression of his own needs. The abuse also contributed to his repressed affect and emotional numbness when faced with conflict. The sexual abuse induced heightened feelings of inadequacy. His history of unreliable and ineffectual social support contributed to his perception that he can trust no one to reliably help him without their causing trouble for him.

Attachment: Damon's father maintained a presence in Damon's life and superficially behaved responsibly—he kept a household for Damon. But this constancy was disrupted by the changing live-in partners and abusive outbursts, inducing ambivalence and insecurity in Damon. He is unstably attached to his parents and yearns for an attached relationship, thus he was highly dependent on his wife and tried to play an idealized role in his marital household. He imagined that having a baby would signify a stronger commitment to their relationship. But his entire history, except for his exposure to the stable life of his aunt, involves women who leave. He was insecurely attached to his wife and fraught with anxiety over the probability that she would leave him. He perceived losing her as his fault, proving that he is a failure as a husband.

Social learning: As the youngest child in a large interactive extended family, Damon learned to be dependent on others while dreading their criticism. While he was trying to live as a competent husband, he showed weak skills because he had never seen them modeled for him, given that his father was such an ineffectual and abusive example. In addition, the predominant conflict resolution mode he witnessed as a child was alcohol and drug use and explosive outbursts by his father. Being male, he would identify strongly with his father.

Biosocial behavior: Being in a state of methamphetamine withdrawal increased his agitation and anxiety. When faced with a socially demanding situation that made him feel like a failure, he was at risk for an angry outburst.

Finally, the social worker offers an interpretive opinion about the social history. The descriptive summary, social functioning assessment, and theory are combined into a theory of the case. In this particular setting, the theory is applied to the issue at hand for the multidisciplinary team, which is Damon's state of mind at the time of the offense.

Case Theory

Damon, who adored his wife but was becoming overwhelmed and frustrated by household and job responsibilities, was worried that his wife was about to leave him, based on recent conversations and arguments. Damon, whose social functioning is impaired by his insecurities and fear of rejection, desperately wanted Tawanna to stay and when she rejected his sexual advances and desire to make a baby, he felt defeated and worthless, causing his anxiety to increase. In an agitated state of drug withdrawal, resorting to maladaptive behavior he acquired through social learning in his father's household, Damon shoved and hit Tawanna. He seems to have lost rational thought because he didn't consider logical alternatives (e.g., leaving the house for a while so he could calm down himself, going to visit his aunt for advice). He psychologically withdrew from the situation, a coping pattern he had learned, shutting out conscious perception of feelings, as he continued to assault his wife. When he realized that she was immobile, Damon realized what he had done and was immediately flooded with emotions: grief, remorse, and fear of punishment.

Again, this example is not a complete report, but an excerpt intended to illustrate how the professional can interpret the social aspects of a life history as they pertain to a particular purpose (in this case, forensic assessment of competence subsequent to a spousal homicide).

The social history assessment was one foundation for a determination by the court that Damon was competent to stand trial—that is, he did know right from wrong, although he was under a drug-induced psychosis at the time of the crime. Damon confessed to his guilt, and the social history assessment was introduced by the defense attorney in court as part of mitigation evidence along with a psychiatric assessment, a neuropsychological assessment, and an educational assessment regarding his learning disability.

Case 2: Example of Descriptive and Interpretive Portions of a Report: Excerpt From Therapist's Assessment Report in a Mental Health Treatment Setting

The second case illustrates a more narrative approach to reporting a social history. In this case, the client is hospitalized for an extended period and a comprehensive multidisciplinary assessment is under way. The social worker who conducted this assessment will use the information in mental health treatment planning. Many of the themes will be explored as a foundation for helping the client to recover from her disorder. As with the first example, this one is partial, based on excerpts from the case record. It is rather lengthy because the intent here is to illustrate the way the professional thinks about the case. The history starts with a summary of key events in the life of Emma's parents before her birth. A genogram to accompany this case is found in Chapter 6 (see Figure 6.2).

Case synopsis: Ms. Blane, age 54, was admitted to a behavioral health center for inpatient hospitalization after being found by police wandering along a highway at night. At first they thought she was intoxicated, but closer examination indicated she was delusional, convinced that she was a 30-year-old mother who had to find her baby. Her identity was matched to that of a missing person based on a report filed by her son. Within two days after hospitalization, Ms. Blane was lucid again and confused about what happened.

Part One: Excerpts From Case Chronology (History Description)

Emma McColl Sims Watson Blane
Abbreviated Life Chronology
Pre-birth–parental history

[Sources: Interview with Emma Blane; interview with Jeffrey Blane (son); interview with Celia McColl Rider (younger sister)]

1946 Emma's mother, Sandra Watson, was only 15 years old when she married Benton McColl, age 19. Both lived in the rural tobacco farming community of Hampton, GA.

Sandra was the daughter of Vernon, a farmer with a "drinking problem." He got drunk about once a week and often became violent against everyone in the household when he was drunk. He would use belts, his fist, cords, a shaving strap, and other objects to hit his wife and the children. Sandra's mother, Anne, was quite submissive and tried to get everyone to stay out of their way. Over time, she started staying in bed much of the time when her husband was out of the house; she never smiled and showed signs of what would be diagnosed today as depression. Sandra spent many Saturday nights in a closet, trying to hide. When Sandra was about seven years old, her mother started working an evening shift at the local mill. Soon after, her father began sexually assaulting her while her mother was at work. This continued until she left to marry Benton.

Benton also suffered abuse at the hands of his father. His family adhered to a strict fundamentalist religious regimen, including hour-long Bible readings each evening. When the children became weary, they would be beaten for closing their eyes or yawning. Benton started staying in town with an older cousin, where he could hang out with other young guys and work at the mill. He met Sandra at his cousin's house when she came to babysit his cousin's children. His family was furious when he and Sandra ran away to be married because they regarded her family as "trash."

1947 Within a year of the marriage, Sandra and Benton began having children. By then, Benton had become disillusioned with Sandra, who was young and struggling to learn to keep house. Benton often slapped or shoved Sandra when something irritated him, such as her overcooking his eggs. Sandra's own mother was too depressed or busy working to give her much guidance or assistance.

1950 In 1950 Sandra bore their third child, a girl, who was premature and died within days of her birth. Sandra developed severe depression and could hardly get out of bed. This irritated Benton immensely so he would often beat her viciously, such as whipping her with a belt while she lay in bed and pursuing her as she tried to get up and do her housework. About this time, Benton, who was still working in the mill, decided to start a church in their neighborhood. He was capable of preaching in the tradition of his family's church, which was generally about sin, condemnation, repentance, and salvation. He insisted Sandra and the children come with him to services twice on Sunday and on Wednesday and Friday evenings. Sandra was responsible for keeping the converted warehouse clean for services.

Before Emma was born, the family demonstrated certain social competencies and vulnerabilities. From a strengths perspective, the families showed intent to be committed through marriage, strong work ethic, and provision of a stable household. Unfortunately these were offset by brutality and sexual exploitation, rigid patriarchy, oppression of women, maternal depression, paternal hypocrisy, and fear of shame in their cultural community. Just before Emma was born her mother was dealing with unresolved grief related to loss of an infant child.

1951 On April 16 Emma was born. She has two older brothers.

About this time Benton became involved with a young woman who lived on her own and supported herself by sewing in her home. Emma's mother and entire family did not know of Benton's relationship with Joanna until Emma was about ten years old. In later life, Benton declared that Joanna had always been the love of his life but that the Bible forbids divorce so he had to stay married to Sandra.

1952 Benton and Joanna have the first of their five children.

1953 Emma's only sister, Celia, the last of Benton and Sandra's children, is born. Benton essentially ignored Celia all her life, giving her neither positive nor negative attention. Benton regularly yelled at Emma and her brothers, calling them "heathens" and beating them cruelly with straps and belts, sometimes drawing blood. He also continued to beat Sandra regularly, snarling at her and once threatening her with a knife.

1961 Emma overheard her mother talking to a coworker about Benton's relationship with Joanna. She walked across town and looked at the little house where Joanna lived. From a distance, she saw her father on the porch playing and laughing with a baby. She had never seen her father smile in her own home. Benton's congregation seemed to tolerate his relationship with Joanna, though he rarely was seen at her house during the daytime. He preached about reaching out to widows and orphans.

The history continues with themes of male infidelity and female fidelity added to those listed earlier. To help the reader understand the subsequent social history report, given that the chronology is cut short here, what follows is an abbreviated time line of other key events in Ms. Blane's life. The chronology includes narrative information explaining the meanings attributed by informants to the events while a time line simply lists the major events.

1967	At age 16, Emma McColl marries Jeff Sims
1968	Son Jeffrey born
1968	Brother's suicide
1969	Daughter Rose born
1974	Father leaves mother; divorce 1975
1975	Jeff left; Emma's first divorce 1977
1979	Father remarries
1982	Emma marries Raeford Watson

1984	Son James born
1988	Daughter Rose's first marriage; son Jeffrey marries
1989	Rose gives birth to Emma's first grandchild
1990	Rose's second child
1992	Raeford leaves; Emma's second divorce 1994
1993	Rose divorces
1995	Rose remarries; Jeffrey's first child born
1999	Father (Benton) dies; Rose's third child born
2002	Mother (Sandra) dies
2003	Rose divorces; Jeffrey's second child born
2004	Married Mac Blane, he left after six months; Jeffrey separates from his wife

Part Two: Excerpts From Social History Assessment (Interpretation)

Following is an excerpt from a report that was filed in preparation for an interdisciplinary case staffing.

July 15, 2005
Social History Assessment
re: **Emma** McColl Sims Watson **Blane**, b. April 16, 1951
I conducted a social history assessment for 54-year-old Emma Blane as a part of her mental health assessment while hospitalized at Murray Behavioral Health Center subsequent to a delusional episode that caused her to be missing for two days. On June 4, 2005, she was found by police wandering along a rural road at night. At first they thought she was intoxicated but upon closer attention realized she believed she was a 30-year-old mother looking for her lost child. Her description matched that in a missing person report filed by her son, Jeffrey, who realized she was missing when he went to pick up his two-year-old from her care. She left the child unattended. The child seems to have eaten Cheerios and played in the vicinity of the grandmother's bed. Physical examination revealed no overt harm to the child.

This assessment is based on

– Review of records and written materials [list would be attached]
– Personal interviews with and observations of Ms. Blane
– Personal interviews with family members [list would be attached]

This report has three sections:

1. Summary of findings
2. Discussion of findings
3. Attachments:
   a. Genogram (family tree)
   b. Chart synopsis of childhood events and adult social functioning
   c. Summary of previous psychiatric reports
   d. Chronology of key life events
   e. Social history assessment
   f. List of records and interviews

1. Summary of findings

This history reveals that Ms. Blane is suffering negative effects of childhood trauma and deprivation that have persisted throughout her life and are clearly contributing to social dysfunction and emotional distress at this time of her life. She has shown remarkable fortitude for much of her life, exerting considerable effort to care for her children and grandchildren and to maintain an organized and socially productive life.

The childhood events include chronic paternal terrorism; extreme fluctuations and discrepancies in paternal moral behavior; maternal depression; paternal rejection; and shame within their faith community. The impact of these events on the child Emma were exacerbated by (1) inadequate protective, coping, and social supports; (2) cultural factors related to religiosity, gender roles, and consistent residence in a small community; and (3) birth order (she was oldest daughter and obliged to care for her mother). According to psychiatrists and psychologists who have evaluated her over the past ten years, prior to this episode, Ms. Blane's unresolved and untreated reactions to these life conditions led to symptoms in adulthood that included chronic depression, stress-related physical ailments, obsessive-compulsive disorder, and dependent personality disorder.

2. Discussion of findings

The following comments are based on information contained in the attachments listed above; they are integral to this discussion.

Recent stressors

Ms. Blane is a 54-year-old woman who lives alone in Hampton, GA. She has been separated since Christmas (about 7 months) from her third husband, Mac Blane. He left just before the holidays. He is purported to be living with another woman at this time. Ms. Blane was the primary financial provider because Mac, a carpenter, has an expensive gambling habit and has drained their resources.

Ms. Blane has experienced several major life stressors in the past two years, including:

– separation from husband Mac
– death of her mother after a long illness, during which Ms. Blane was her primary caregiver
– fear that her daughter Rose had cancer (tests revealed no malignancy)
– her daughter Rose's second divorce and need for Emma's help with child care
– her son Jeffrey's wife, who has bipolar disorder, faced criminal charges for passing bad checks; they separated and also needed Emma's help to care for their children
– relocation from her house of ten years to a mobile home on a lot adjacent to her adult daughter, Rose
– development of carpal tunnel syndrome, for which she had surgery and filed a worker's compensation claim that her employer denied
– resignation from her job a week before the delusional episode
– extended psychiatric outpatient care, started in 1999 for reasons of suicidal depression and associated physical ailments

Critical facts from the history

In general, Ms. Blane's functioning throughout her adulthood has been characterized by notable responsibility for her family, church, and job. She is devoted to her daughter and sons, having provided them with nurture throughout their childhoods and maintaining daily contact with them by phone or visit in their adulthood. She keeps a tidy home, enjoys cooking, and gives her children guidance and opportunities. Her children have in turn become responsible family and community members. Ms. Blane does, however, have difficulty promoting their independence as adolescents and adults, insisting that she be involved in all their life decisions.

Ms. Blane has been married twice before. She was only 16 when she married her first husband, Jeff Sims, father of Jeffrey and Rose. He quickly became routinely violent against her and the children as they came. Emma coped by praying a lot and trying to please him. After ten years, he left her to live with his current wife in the community where Emma lives. Jeffrey and Rose still visit him occasionally.

When she was 31 Ms. Blane married Raeford Watson, a trucker, age 46. She says she was madly in love with him and felt safe for the first time in her life. He was away for weeks at a time, which she did not mind. They have one son. In 1992 Raeford left, telling Emma she was clingy and manipulative. Their son James stayed with Rae whenever he was in town; they are still quite close.

Ms. Blane has practiced her religion throughout her adulthood, attending multiple church services weekly and all special church events when possible. She encourages others close to her to become involved in the church.

Ms. Blane has been a devoted Angier Mills employee for most of her life, having risen through the ranks to a position in management support. She regarded Angier as a family for her, a place where many of her coworkers were friends. She had a commendable performance history with the company. She worked long hours, including weekends, as necessary.

Ms. Blane's social activities involve her children and grandchildren, siblings, church members, and coworkers. She is regarded as particularly available and helpful when any of these familiar persons confronted illness or distress. She helps clean house, cook, run errands, and bring cheer when needed.

Ms. Blane has lived in the vicinity of Hampton all her adult life, first in the home of her in-laws, then in a rental home with Jeff and her children, next in a home she had built, and finally in a mobile home. Most of Ms. Blane's extended family has also lived in the general vicinity of Hampton all this time.

Social context of mental health problems

Although Ms. Blane has led a highly functional and productive life, she has faced numerous extraordinary stressors, discussed below. Records and interviews indicate that at several periods in her life Ms. Blane has been affected by mental health problems that inhibit her daily living and influence her life decisions. Most notably, these problems include severe depression, noted in medical records in 1979 (subsequent to her first divorce and her father's remarriage) and again in 1990, when she had an abortion after an extramarital affair and her husband was ill. She also has had incontinence since childhood and gastrointestinal problems that seem to be influenced by her mental condition.

These symptoms suggest that beneath her responsible, caregiving personality was chronic depression and emotional distress associated with persistent anxiety, insecurity, dependence, passivity, feelings of inadequacy and inferiority, need to be regarded as competent, and need for affection. Eight independent psychological and psychiatric assessments at three points in time (1979–1980, 1990, 2000) reveal similar symptoms, indicating these are persistent traits, not situational reactions.

Close examination, through the assessments and interviews with family members, reveals that the need for order and conformity in Ms. Blane's life is extreme. She has rigid behavioral expectations of herself and others, avoids conflict and anger, works to the point of exhaustion to please others, insists on stability, and requires order and control in the environments of which she is a part.

Ms. Blane regards herself as highly self-sufficient although she is excessively dependent on her adult children, insisting that they be dependent on her.

Ms. Blane regards men as powerful and seeks their protection while working to avoid upsetting them. Yet she mistrusts them, anticipates their violations of the moral code of her culture, and expects to be disappointed by them. She is dependent on men and has engaged in a series of attempted long-term relationships, including three marriages and several other partnerships.

Ms. Blane expects women to be inadequate, in need of guidance and protection, and morally superior to men. Ms. Blane dreads feeling humiliated or ashamed and has spent a large part of her life "putting on a happy face." She minimizes extraordinarily violent and immoral conduct by her father, denies bizarre behavior that may appear to be mental illness, and tries to avoid disclosure of her behavior that violates her moral code (e.g., abortion, adultery).

Ms. Blane's behavior as an exceptional caregiver, industrious worker, and rigid moral influence are as much a product of her need to see herself this way as a need to gain recognition from others. Being compulsively good, hardworking, and upright helps to repress underlying emotional chaos and despair that is revealed in psychological testing, reports of her rigid and occasionally bizarre behavior, and inconsistencies between her reported memories of events and the reported memories of others. Ms. Blane's compulsion to repress her emotions has apparently contributed to numerous stress-related physical ailments, including chronic incontinence and diarrhea, sleep disturbances, head- and neck aches, asthma, and exhaustion.

Ms. Blane expresses acute anxiety about the instability in the lives of her daughter Rose and son Jeffrey. Her son James, who has spent less time with her and relates particularly to his father, Raeford, is leading a stable life. The other two have formed maladaptive attachments to spouses and other intimate partners. Ms. Blane feels responsible for their troubles and ashamed that they are struggling. She tries to compensate by being as helpful as possible and does not seem to consider separating herself from their decisions as an option.

Contributing factors from the early history

Research and clinical mental health studies document that all the symptoms exhibited by Ms. Blane are commonly found in adult survivors of unresolved, untreated, severe childhood trauma. A review of Ms. Blane's childhood history suggests a link between her history and her adult functioning. Interviews with Ms. Blane, her son, and her siblings reveal these factors:

1. Domestic terrorism. Emma was born into a home where her mother and older siblings had long coped with her father's terrorism. Emma's father was a tyrant, frequently and unpredictably wielding knives and threatening to kill Emma's mother and all the children. The family members were convinced he would kill them if they failed to comply with his wishes. He specifically prohibited escape by stating he would kill them if his wife tried to leave him. He repeatedly beat his wife and all the older children, including Emma, in ways that exceeded community norms regarding use of force for discipline. He used belts, firewood, fists, and his own force in ways that caused welts and knocked family members down or against walls. He once held a knife to 11-year-old Emma's throat when she tried to intervene in his beating her mother; he grabbed her from behind, paralyzed her movement, and poked the knife several times into her neck and upper chest, causing bleeding, while he said he would kill her.

Emma urinated from terror and subsequently developed a problem with incontinence when under stress, for which she still wears pads now. Emma's mother took her to see a doctor regarding the incontinence; he treated her for infection but it did not stop the problem. Brother Andy was once seen by a doctor for headaches; the explanation was that it was his nerves. As a young adult, sister Celia had a "nervous breakdown" that doctors said was induced by living with her father; her symptoms improved when she moved away. These are all typical reactions of children who are chronically abused or witness domestic violence.

The beatings and verbal abuse were unpredictable; they sometimes occurred in the middle of the night, when the father would awaken the children. When he came home they never knew if he would be in a temper or not. He imposed rigid expectations on their behavior. Emma would sometimes hide under the house or in the yard while her father was beating her mother.

By the time Emma was born, her mother had apparently given up any effort to escape. Her older brothers moved away from home as soon as they could to get away. The family regarded the father as all-powerful. Prior to Emma's birth, her father had demonstrated, from the family's perspective, that he could control not only the home but also the church, where he was an occasional minister, and the legal system, where his father was the jailer. His wife once tried to seek financial support when he abandoned them through the court. He returned home, only to be more violent, apparently angered by their efforts to hold him accountable. By the time Emma was born, her mother had adopted the routine of trying to keep her husband satisfied by being withdrawn and compliant and seeking solace from her faith and religious practice. Even before their independence, Emma's brothers were allowed to engage in neighborhood activities that took them away from the house, but the girls were expected to stay at home except for church, school, and special activities like bowling, for which they had to have specific permission.

Emma's mother was forced into silence, compliance, and conflict avoidant behavior to avert her husband's violence or attempts to kill her or the children. She was unable to protect herself or her children and perceived that the church and legal system were unavailable for protection because of her husband's alignment with them. For reasons noted below, she also could not look to neighbors for protection, and her extended family was ineffective. Following her mother's survival pattern, Emma learned early to be compliant, nonassertive with men, and compulsive about creating order in environments so temper would not arise. She was known for her good cheer, attempts to make people happy, housekeeping, and care for her younger sister to ease her mother's strain. Emma aligned with her mother in anticipating her father's rage and doing whatever was necessary to avert it. This pattern of fearing male rage became a part of her.

Emma has long yearned for a male protector. As a teen, she thought she had found one in Jeff, whom she married. Within months, though, his abuse and threats to her life began. She found herself in the role her mother had long lived: silently submissive, trying to keep the peace, providing for the family while her husband indulged his vices. Jeff's religious conversion and subsequent responsible behavior seemed only to elicit anxiety in Emma, who found his conversion hard to trust because her father's had been so unreliable.

In desperation, Emma learned to seek a sense of security by keeping her life as stable and predictable as possible.

2. Rejection. Emma and her family members still yearn for their deceased father's love, stating, with tears, "I don't know why Daddy didn't love me (us)." They note he could be charming with people outside the home, especially during the periods when he was a minister. They admired his preaching talent and power. Emma seems to feel not that she was actively disliked, but that she was insignificant, expendable in his eyes. No matter how hard she tried, she could not please him—he always indicated what she did was wrong. Unlike her brother Andy, who tried to forget his father ("I acted like he was dead") after he left home, Emma never stopped trying to win his affection. She had always hoped he would repent and return to her mother after he left her, but his remarriage showed that he did not intend to do so.

Emma identifies with her mother, who was rejected by Emma's father when he chose other women. While Emma was growing up he maintained a relationship with another woman who lived in their community; she bore him five children who recognized him as their father. He also had other affairs and eventually abandoned Emma's mother, divorced her, and married another.

Emma's mother was devoted to her family, but emotionally distant. She nursed their physical ailments but their emotional distress was not discussed. Battered women often discourage their children from expressing their emotions, in part because it might upset their father and precipitate an attack and in part because they feel emotionally overwhelmed and helpless themselves.

Emma thus learned to behave in ways that would make her feel less isolated, unattractive, unworthy, and insignificant. She maintains an attractive appearance, was socially active, worked hard, and provided committed care to others. She likes to be needed. She also learned to hide her distress. She became extremely dependent on family relationships to gain assurance that she is wanted and needed.

3. Moral inconsistencies. This pattern is among the more unusual and profound in Ms. Blane's life history. Her father's fluctuations were extreme, shifting from periods of sanctimonious behavior, including church ministry, to multiple moral transgressions. The record indicates that at various times he was a thief, a repeated adulterer practicing a bigamist-type relationship, a gambler, violent and neglectful husband and father, and occasional drunkard. Exposure to these fluctuations had powerful significance for Emma, who grew up attending church with her mother, whose faith and moral compliance never wavered. They attended a fundamentalist Protestant church that gave them a sense of being in a caring community and protected from forces in the "outside" world. The church has strict behavioral expectations and a theology that emphasizes hell and damnation for violators. The church advocated repentance and forgiveness. Her father publicly repented several times, but inevitably "slid back." The family took pride in him during the periods when he was a preacher and yearned for his permanent conversion, but Emma learned to mistrust his ability to maintain the righteous life. Though he repented often, he never told his family he was sorry for the harm he had done to them.

The intermittent nature of negative behavior induces anticipatory anxiety and learned helplessness. If Emma's father had been "all bad," consistently immoral and rejecting of the church, the family could have coped by accepting the worst and learning to live with it. Instead, he had good periods, when the family would forgive him and feel affiliated with his charm, stature in the church, and relative peace in the household. Chronic victims of intermittent family violence often feel worse during these good periods than the bad periods, because the bad is unpredictable and anxiety about when the good will turn bad starts to escalate. The victim becomes vigilant, anticipating the worst and mistrusting the good intentions.

The church teachings and her parent's behavior significantly affected Emma's gender role expectations and perceptions. The church taught that women should be submissive and that men should be protectors and providers. Emma's mother was submissive; she had to idealize, though, what her father could be like. It also taught that all members should try to behave properly; in Emma's experience, only her mother could do that; her father could not. Emma and her mother had to assume the provider role for their families. Emma learned to expect disappointment in relationships with men.

Emma grew up learning to fear damnation for her transgressions and also to fear her father's wrath. Although her father himself did not comply, he expected his children to live by a strict moral and behavioral code. An apparent lesson in this pattern is that men are free to do as they please, then they can repent and be saved. Women are not free, must be as right-eous as possible, and should help lead men to righteousness. When men ask for forgiveness, women must give it, although Emma also notes that "apologies mean nothing" because of her experiences with men. Emma learned to appear right (and righteous) in her words and deeds.

4. Shame. The family grew up in a mill village, where almost everyone was working poor. The families had mutual support systems (e.g., shared child care, played group games, helped each other in times of illness and death) and tended to know one another. One of the worst labels a family in this community could have would be to be called "dirt" or "trash." Even today members of the family can barely say the words, because there were peri-ods when they felt they were regarded as such, when their father failed to support the family. Before Emma's birth, they were on welfare while the father was away on an adulterous affair. Once, when Emma was about 10, they lived in a shack, a dwelling substandard to other village homes.

They also feel profound shame over their father's immoral behavior, which was humiliatingly known to people in the community. Their church's admonition to avoid evil was also hard to do when a major transgressor was their own father—so they felt guilt and shame by association. Emma's father and her husband made the family conspirators to their immoral ways: her father forced her mother to give him money to support his bad habits, just as Jeff made Emma spend her money on his gambling debts; Jeff made her pose for photographs in a bathing suit, though she was raised to believe bathing suits were sinful; and when Jeff was impotent Emma felt forced into sexual acts that she regards as inappropriate.

The family copes by emphasizing the positive aspects of their life and minimizing the negative. They also work hard to comply with their moral code to avoid shame.

Another factor that appears to be present in this family is the tendency to minimize the severity of their father's abuse. This is typical of abuse survivors, who seem unaware that people who have not experienced abuse might regard the behavior as extreme. A key factor in the tendency to minimize is that the abuser has communicated messages to the child victim that the abuse was the victim's fault, in some way, so the person tends to minimize to avoid beliefs about his or her own contribution to the undesirable situation.

Emma learned to minimize guilt and shame she felt about her own behavior that violated her moral code. For example, she had a therapeutic abortion (which she now believes is immoral), but she offers an explanation of it that involves her doubt that she was pregnant and her need for gynecological treatment at the time. She avoids discussing the sexual aspects of her relationships with any of her husbands.

Associated with being "dirt" is the notion that people who are dirt are poorer than others for reasons of wrong moral choices. Emma, like her mother, has thus worked hard to maintain her family's financial security so that she will not be seen as poor.

5. Inadequate protection and coping support. Confronted with persistent terror, rejection, moral confusion, and shame, the child Emma had few supports to mediate the harmful impacts. Sometimes abused children have an outlet, such as an involved aunt or teacher who assures them of their worth and comforts their distress. Emma was essentially alone. Her mother, as noted above, gave comfort but was unable to protect her. The older children had tried to fight back and, in the early years, her mother had. But by the time Emma came along, her mother was in a compliant pattern that encouraged silence and solitary coping. Emma's siblings adopted this as well, as they note, "We had it buried until Emma did this" [referring to the dissociative episode and endangerment of her grandchild].

Emma's older siblings gave some protection and comfort while she was very young by taking the brunt of her father's abuse, but when she grew older, they moved away. After the brothers started staying away from home, the abuse of Emma escalated. By then, the only persons at home with the father were female: Emma's mother, Emma, and a sister two years younger.

Emma reports no one outside the family to whom she could turn for comfort. Her mother's family lived at a distance. Shame kept Emma and her mother from revealing the struggles they confronted at home. Her father was aligned with the men who led the church.

Emma learned the family pattern of silence, minimization of threat, and mutual dependence among vulnerable persons. In the face of the real threats she encountered, these coping styles were unlikely to reduce her anxiety. The appearance of depression and somatic problems is common under such conditions.

6. Cultural factors. The impact of Emma's childhood trauma and deprivation was shaped to some extent by the cultural factors of religiosity, gender role expectations, and mill town culture. She had to learn to handle persistent discrepancies between what she believed should be and what really was.

As noted above, the nature of Emma's religious upbringing encouraged rigid compliance, avoidance of shame, endurance of life's challenges, and hard work to help others lead a righteous life. Challenging authority (such as her father) was discouraged. Yet she had to cope with the ambivalence of her father's inconsistent moral behavior and the righteous life she thought he should, and believed he could, lead. This childhood pattern has been repeated in the lives of men with whom she has formed relationships. Her father was a minister who had been unfaithful to his wife for years. Her husband Jeff went to church, then backslid as a gambler and abuser, then was saved. Raeford had been a gambler and divorcee; then he was saved. Mr. Walker, her work supervisor, is a church deacon and a man with authority in her workplace, which had taken care of her; yet he has been lecherous toward her and other women. These relationships with men who had engaged in immoral conduct and then been saved would predictably elicit the ambivalence, mistrust, and anticipatory fear of her father that Emma had learned as a child.

Similarly, she was raised to regard women as submissive and nurturing and men as protective and providing, but her father's violence and neglect created a conflict for her between the ideal and the real. She yearned for the ideal protective and providing relationship with a man while doing her own protecting and providing for her family. She had learned she could not trust men to fulfill their roles. Her church taught her to honor marriage, but her experience with marriage (her parents,' her own, her children's, and her siblings') has taught her that conflict and disappointment are inevitable and that protection is unlikely.

Within a small, familiar area such as a mill village, families learn to avoid shame by hiding what they believe should be family secrets. Young Emma thus had to learn to act as if her home life was orderly and pure when in fact it was tainted by her father's chaotic outbursts and sinful ways. Emma continued to live in the same relatively small community with stable social networks throughout her life. Her mother and father, though divorced, were never far from her. She kept her children near her even in adulthood. She apparently never considered leaving, although distance might have given her an opportunity for relief from distress associated with early experiences. She was highly dependent on the stability of her small world, which is understandable given her passivity and emotional needs.

In the old mill village, the employer was regarded paternalistically, as the giver of care to the employees. Emma carried this view of employer to her work; she regarded Angier Mills as a family. When her employer denied her health claim, she felt abandoned by a group that had been, from her perspective, a caring family.

Conclusion. Ms. Blane's life story indicates that she suffers lifelong negative effects of childhood trauma and deprivation that are related to the social dysfunction and emotional distress in her life at the present time. The childhood events include chronic paternal terrorism and parental moral inconsistencies, rejection, and shame. The impact of these events on the child Emma has been exacerbated by inadequate social supports and cultural factors. According to previous mental health evaluations, Ms. Blane suffered chronic depression, stress-related physical ailments, and dependent personality disorder.

During her adult life, Ms. Blane has appeared to be well adjusted most of the time: She was financially secure, actively involved in family and church, and in positions of relatively high status within her social networks. Early in her life she learned to hide to escape life-threatening challenges, to pretend that she was happy so her needs would not aggravate others, and to please others in order to feel valued. As long as Ms. Blane's life was simple and predictable, her inner turmoil and despair were contained. When confronted by multiple life changes, the chaos within Ms. Blane began to emerge. Her repressed feelings of overwhelming despair, abandonment, and threat of extermination began to emerge in the form of depression, incontinence and diarrhea (loss of control), and attempts to change her environment to reduce her discomfort.

The social history assessment was used as a basis for diagnosing Emma's severe depression with dissociative symptoms. A psychiatrist prescribed medication. The social worker who wrote the assessment was the primary counseling therapist for Ms. Blane and relied on the assessment as a way to focus many of the topics that she and Emma discussed, particularly given that Emma had a tendency to minimize and deny certain emotions. The assessment crystallized certain themes and served as a guide for therapeutic goal setting (which was done together with Emma) and action.

Putting It All Together

The social history assessment typically is part of a broader process that leads to a decision or course of action aimed at a positive outcome. The social history assessment, together with other information about how a person functions biologically and psychologically, can help explain why a person behaves, thinks, or feels a certain way. Given that all lives are in progress, still forming, a careful review of history can provide insight into how to approach the future. The person may seek to strengthen certain areas or change habits or patterns that have harmed development. He or she can build on positive themes and change negative themes.

Each person is unique but not alone. By working with a professional who understands human behavior through case experience and knowledge of theory and research, a person can realize untapped potential and release fresh capacity to manage life problems.

Note

1. The cases presented in this chapter are based on real-life situations although identifying information and settings have been changed to protect the privacy of the individuals involved. The thematic content is true to the assessments that were actually conducted.

6

Tools to Aid Social History Development

Tools are mere supports for the professional's knowledge of social science and skills in the art of assessing, interpreting, and explaining human behavior in a the social environment. Tools cannot do the work or guide the process. Given that caveat, what follows are several tools useful in the development of social histories. They include the following:

- Social History Interview Topical Guide
- Sample Family Social History Assessment Instruments
- Checklist for Social History Records Compilation
- Tools to describe social relationships:
  - Genogram
  - Sociogram or ecomap

- Tools to describe life events:
  - Chronology
  - Life history calendar
  - Time line
  - Photographs and artifacts

- Tools to describe life context:
  - Geographic maps, building plans, and other drawings
  - Community/neighborhood profile
  - Ecological chart

- Figures to illustrate theories

The tools in the latter part of the chapter that involve drawing figures rely, intentionally, on MSWord™ because of its simplicity and wide availability. Professionals with more time can acquire more sophisticated software for drawing figures and charts. Professionals with less time can use old-fashioned sketching by hand to portray ideas.

In addition, *My History Is America's History,* a handbook produced by the National Endowment for the Humanities (1999), provides a helpful framework for putting a family history together.

Social History Interview Topical Guide

Social histories are long and complicated. The list below, "Topics to Cover in a Social History Interview," reminds the interviewer to explore comprehensive aspects of the life. This array of topics should be covered through discussions with multiple interviewees, including the person who is the subject of the history and those people who know the person best. Every item need not be covered for every person, but, somehow, the many parts should be covered and integrated into a whole.

First, a few notes about the interview process. The list, which is gleaned from several sources as well as personal experience, is not intended to be used as a questionnaire. Interviewees generally like to tell the story in their own words, with a few relevant open-ended prompts from the interviewer. So the interviewer may keep the checklist at hand and periodically glance at it to ensure topics are being covered.

A few process reminders:

- *Follow principles of empathic and effective interviewing.* Use responsive listening techniques throughout the interview. Observe the interviewee's behaviors and apparent emotions. Gently probe for details. Be comfortable with silence. Show sensitivity and respect even when the interviewee discusses disturbing or outrageous topics (e.g., while listening to a father lie about how he never molested his children, or listening to one tell in detail how he did molest them).
- *Build trust and rapport with the informant.* Start with basic chit-chat. Then introduce yourself, your role, and what you plan to do during the interview. Maintain respectful eye contact. Show emotional warmth. Make no judgments about the information.

- *Address issues of race, ethnicity, religion, sexual orientation, and socioeconomic class competently.* Match interviewer to respondent as closely as possible and use sharp skills for building bridges where matches cannot be.
- *Gather the information from multiple informants.* Each person who experiences a shared life event will recall it somewhat differently. Who remembers what says much about a family.
- *Gather sensitive information over more than one session.* Interviewees are unlikely to reveal highly sensitive information, particularly topics dealing with sexuality, money, or crime, at a first interview. They need time to reflect on the process of the first interview and to develop confidence in the interviewer.
- *Use mostly open-ended questions.* Open-ended questions elicit emotions and, based on what the informant chooses to say, tell you about his or her personality. The exceptions are people who have limited communication or cognitive skills and those with high anxiety; they will respond more effectively to simple closed-ended questions to which they can give short answers. Closed-ended questions are helpful for gathering specific details, such as names, locations, or ages, from anyone.

  A general tip about open-ended questions is that if they can be answered with "yes" or "no," they are not good open-ended questions. For example, "Do you love your mom?" will not elicit as detailed a response as, "Tell me how you feel about your mom" or, "What is your earliest memory of your mom?" followed by, "What else do you remember about her?" and, "How did you feel about that?" None of the latter four questions could have a "yes" or "no" response.
- *Go for the whole truth.* This means capturing the bad as well as the good stories. The idea is to develop full understanding.
- *Avoid interviews with multiple informants at the same time, except for limited periods.* Brief periods to observe the interactions among multiple family members or others can provide useful information about the social dynamics of the person's networks. The substance of the information tends to become clouded or intentionally obscured, however, when people communicate it in front of one another. Interview one person at a time.

- *Make copious notes.* Record the information in the words of the informant. Keep a marginal set of brief memos to yourself as your interpretive thoughts are triggered and themes emerge.
- *Always close the interview with gratitude for the interviewee's helpfulness.*

Topics to Cover in a Social History Interview

In conducting a social history, the following topics should be explored. This is a list of topics—not an interview protocol. The skilled interviewer will create appropriate questions to elicit the information. Sample questions are offered at the end of each section. These do not constitute a comprehensive list of questions. They are illustrative of how the interviewer might elicit some of the information on the topics list.

As with any life history, attention should be given to these factors *at various developmental stages* (prenatal, infancy, early childhood, school-age years, early and late adolescence, adulthood). The *ecological context* (family/caregivers, peer group, neighborhood, broader community) should also be assessed. *Cultural relevance* is also critical for determining whether the child was relatively deprived.

COVER

Interviewer's name

Interviewee's name

Others present

Date/time

Location

FAMILY BACKGROUND

FAMILY COMPOSITION

Gather the following information for client, mother, mother figures, father, father figures, grandmothers, grandfathers, great-grandmothers, great-grandfathers, brothers, sisters (full, half, step), and their descendents.

Also include client's spouse(s) or co-parent and offspring. Include former family members (i.e., those divorced), household members, adoptees, foster children, and people who are considered members of the family even if there is no biological or legal link.

For each:

Name

Date of birth

Place of birth

Gender

Race/ethnic identification

Religious identification and affiliation

Educational attainment

Occupation

Marital status

Any special conditions (e.g., intellectual impairment, mental illness, addiction)

Complete the genogram as you gather this information (see guide for genograms later in this chapter).

PRE-BIRTH FAMILY

- Circumstances around parents' meeting; nature and extent of their relationship
- Circumstance around conception of client (planned?)
- If parents were married, circumstances of marriage
- Parents' relationships with own parents, in-laws, and extended family
- Mother's pre-pregnancy health status (Age? Health conditions? Used tobacco? Used alcohol or drugs?)
- Mother's health during pregnancy (Health care? Complications? e.g., bleeding, illness, toxemia, prescription drugs during pregnancy or birth process, smoking, alcohol or drug use? Suffer injuries during pregnancy? Stress level?)

- Preparation for childbirth (e.g., Classes? Prepare clothing, place for baby?)
- Major events in the community, the nation, or the world at this time?

Sample questions:
What have you been told about what was happening in your family before you were born?
As far as you know, how did your parents meet?

CHILDHOOD DEVELOPMENTAL HISTORY

BIRTH

- Complications (e.g., full term or premature, respiratory difficulties, jaundice, birth defects, fever)
- Mother's condition immediately after birth (Complications? Fatigue? Depression?)
- Social support at and in weeks after birth
- Breastfeeding
- Health condition and early health care
- Primary caregiver of the child
- Quality of family residence, sources of income
- Quality of parents' relationship
- Birth order; siblings, any miscarriages, stillbirths, or loss of other children

Sample questions:
What do you know about the circumstances around your birth?
Please share with me some of your family's stories about you as a baby.

ALL AGES (birth–18)

Note information about these topics will change over the child's life span—a thorough history will record all answers at each age or stage

- Household composition
  - Who lived with the child?
  - Primary caregiver of the child; quality of nurture

- Quality of parents' relationship, whether together or not
- Supervision and developmental support
  - o Child care arrangements while parents at work or unavailable; quality of care
  - o Parents' involvement in child's daily life; routine, for example, were meals served (how many per day?), bedtime, activities
  - o Discipline techniques; was punishment appropriate to age and offense? Treated similar to siblings?

- Signs of abuse, neglect, or sexual exploitation
- Nutrition
  - o Type and amounts of food—adequate nourishment?
  - o Eating habits of the family; for example, congregate meals or independent eating by different family members
  - o Any atypical eating patterns; for example, over-eating or under-eating

- Housing
  - o Quality of family residence; for example, plumbing, utilities, leaks, bugs or vermin, in need of repair
  - o Changes in residence
  - o Personal space: Where did child sleep? Keep clothes?

- Health
  - o General condition; illnesses; injuries (head injuries in particular)
  - o Health care; medications; dental health care

- Mental health
  - o General condition—temperament; signs of emotional or behavioral problems
  - o Treatment history
  - o How do family members perceive that client handled stress?

- Caregivers' sources of income
- Family social networks
  - o Mother's family and social networks (positive and negative aspects of each)
  - o Father's family and social networks (positive and negative aspects of each)

- Family beliefs
  o Key family beliefs and principles
  o Faith community involvement

- Leisure
  o Typical leisure activities in the family
  o Family special occasions
  o What were holidays like? Vacations?

- Signs of alcohol or drug use by child or any family member
- Any major losses or trauma; for example, death of loved one, parental separation, accident, natural disaster

Sample questions:
What are some of the main events that you remember about your childhood?

Who did you live with as you were growing up? In the early years? During elementary school? As a teenager? What was it like living with _____?

Can you remember a time when you got into trouble? Tell me about it. How did your parent(s) handle it?

ADDITIONAL TOPICS REGARDING EARLY DEVELOPMENT (ages 0–5)

- Milestones (smiling, rolling over, crawling, talking, walking, writing)
- Caregivers' perceptions of baby's temperament
- Toilet training (conditions, age)
- Early childhood program (Home based? Center? School-linked?)
- School readiness

Sample questions:
What was life like for you and your family when you were very young—before you started school?

What is your earliest memory?

ADDITIONAL TOPICS REGARDING
CHILDHOOD (ages 6–11)

- Early education; kindergarten experience
- School enrollment (all schools attended), performance (attendance, academic strengths and weaknesses, age-appropriate progress, behavior problems, parental involvement in school on behalf of the child)
- Special education; other special school support (e.g., free lunch, tutoring)
- Peer relationships (Who? Quality of these relationships?)
- Temperament; typical mood; any signs of depression or suicidality?
- Skills, achievements, extracurricular activities
- Sexual development; onset of puberty; education about sexuality; sexual activity

Sample questions:
Tell me about life with your brothers and sisters when you were a child (age 6–11).
What was elementary school like for you?
How did you feel about being a [boy, girl] at that age?
What did you like best about yourself as a child?
Did someone close to you die while you were young?
Do you recall hearing your parents argue? Tell me about that.

ADDITIONAL TOPICS REGARDING
ADOLESCENCE (ages 12–17)

- Educational participation and performance (attendance, academic strengths and weaknesses, behavior problems, parental involvement in school on behalf of the child)
- Special education; other special school support (e.g., free lunch; tutoring)
- Peer relationships (Who? Quality of these relationships?)
- Mentors; role models—who did the child admire?
- Afterschool activities
- Skills, achievements, extracurricular activities
- Child's employment history, sources of income

- Romantic relationships
- Development of sexual identity
- Sexual development and activity; sex education

Sample questions:

What do you remember most about being a teenager?

Who did you hang out with during your high school years? What did they mean to you?

What were your grades in high school? [If poor performance or failure]: What do you believe led to your performance in school? How did your [primary caregiver] react to your grades?

What values did your parents emphasize to you?

SOCIAL ENVIRONMENT
OF THE FAMILY OF ORIGIN

HOUSEHOLD

- Members of client's households from the time of his or her birth to the time he or she left the household of origin, including family members and others
- Births of siblings (include parental miscarriages, abortions, or stillbirths)
- Describe reasons for changes in the household composition (i.e., death, separation of intimate partners, divorce, incarceration, deployment for military service, absence for employment reasons)
- Who was the functional head of household?

Sample questions:

Who did you live with? Did you ever stay somewhere else?

Who would you say was the head of your household? Tell me about how that person ran the household [or: Tell me how they shared responsibility for the household].

PARENTS/CAREGIVERS

- Major accomplishments
- Social functioning
- Occupation
- Mental health status

- Alcohol or other drug use
- Involvement in criminal activity
- Educational level of each
- Medical conditions, disabilities, or impairments
- Perpetration of violence or sexual abuse
- Victimization
- Coping styles, particularly with regard to how they responded to what happened to their children outside the home

Sample questions:
Who raised you?
How would you describe your parents?
How did your parents respond when you were sick?

OTHER KIN

- Family's involvement with extended family; frequency and nature of contact; mother's regard for father's family; father's regard for mother's family
- Describe any of the following conditions that anyone on the family tree might have:
  - Mental health problem
  - Mental retardation
  - Learning problem
  - Alcohol or other drug use
  - Involvement in criminal activity
  - Medical conditions or disabilities
  - Perpetration of violence or sexual abuse
  - Victimization

Sample questions:
Has anyone in your family tree ever received treatment for a mental health problem?
How did you feel when you knew your _____ (e.g., grandfather) was drunk again?

HOUSING

- List all moves, with dates, that involved relocation of the client
- Physical conditions of the various homes in which the client lived
- Who owned the residence? Rental conditions?

- How did conditions of client's homes compare with conditions of those around it?
- Periods of homelessness or transience (e.g., staying temporarily at others' homes)

Sample questions:
Describe the apartment you lived in when you went to _____ Elementary School. Did the plumbing work?

FAMILY RESOURCES

- List all jobs that each parent held during the client's childhood
- List other sources of income
- How did the family perceive their economic status relative to others?
- How did each parent perceive his or her occupational status?
- Was the family involved in a church or faith community? Participation patterns?

Sample questions:
What sort of work did your mother [father] do?
Compared to other people in your neighborhood, was your family better off or worse off?

FAMILY DYNAMICS

- Emotional support and nurture, expressions of affection. How did the client perceive caregivers' feelings for him or her? How do caregivers report feeling?
- How did caregivers express feelings for client's positive accomplishments?
- How did the family communicate? Solve problems?
- What values did parents seem to emphasize with regard to childrearing?
- Describe fully relationship between client and his mother; other mother figures (e.g., grandmother, stepmother); father; other father figures (e.g., grandfather, stepfather)
- Describe fully the relationship between client and each of his or her siblings, including sexual relations, infliction of physical pain, or manipulation of parents
- Describe fully the relationship between the client and each of the other key household members (e.g., nonparent adults, children who are not kin)

- Authority structure of the family
- Methods of dealing with conflict and anger in the family
- Coalitions among family members
- Family secrets
- Describe fully any harmful dynamics, to include:
  - Excessive discipline and control toward client, toward other children
  - Excessive permissiveness
  - Infliction of physical pain
  - Sexual abuse in any form
  - Emotional abuse
  - Exposure to intimate partner violence

Sample questions:
What do you recall as the best time you ever had with your family?
Did your family ever make you upset or angry?
Did your parent(s) ever hit you? Describe how that would happen.
How did your family communicate? What did you like about your family's communication style? What do you wish had been different?

SEXUAL HISTORY

- Describe how the family handled matters related to sexuality
- Describe first sexual knowledge (e.g., about menstruation, ejaculation, intercourse)
- Describe first sexual experience (include masturbation, relations with others including fondling, various forms of intercourse)
- Describe characteristics of the sexual interaction (e.g., consensual, ambivalent, forced)

Sample questions:
How did you first learn about sexuality?
What were your family's typical ways of communicating about sexual matters?

LEGAL SYSTEM HISTORY

- Client or family members' involvement in
  - Juvenile or criminal justice system
  - Civil justice system (e.g., party to a lawsuit, court-ordered commitment to institution)

o Family court (e.g., divorce, child support, child custody, child protection, termination of parental rights)

TRAUMATIC EVENTS

- Describe any unusual acute or chronic stressors (e.g., perceived or actual threats to life, attempted or actual homicide, attempted or actual suicide, unexpected deaths)
- Describe any significant losses (e.g., beloved family members, pet, friend)
- Major accidents or injuries
- Exposure to natural or technological disaster
- Exposure to community violence
- Exposure to war or civil conflict

Sample questions:
What was the worst experience in your life?
Do you ever have flashbacks, that is, times when you feel like you are reliving that event?
Did anything you valued ever get destroyed or lost?

SOCIAL NETWORKS

- Describe the composition of each parent's friends and social network and how each parent related to them
- Describe the religious affiliation of the family and involvement in religious activities
- Describe the client's social networks
- Describe the client's mentors and role models

Sample questions:
What do you like to do for fun?
Outside your family, who really knows you? What is your relation with (that person)?
Who has influenced your life the most?
Who did your parents spend their time with?

NEIGHBORHOOD/COMMUNITY

- Describe the neighborhoods where the family lived; did they feel like they belonged?
- Describe each school the client attended

Sample questions:

What was your neighborhood like? What did you like about it? Dislike?

ETHNIC/CULTURAL COMMUNITY

- Client's identity in terms of race/ethnicity? How does client feel about this identity? Family's identity?
- Describe the degree of support the client and family perceive from their ethnic/cultural group
- Describe the client's perception of how members of the racial/ethnic group with which he or she identifies related to other groups? Signs of discrimination?
- Family's or individual's religious affiliation; how important is it? Conflict over religious practices? How do religious beliefs influence self-esteem, gender roles, individual identity and development?

Sample questions:

If I ask, "Who are you?" how would you answer?

How do you describe your racial or ethnic identity? How do you feel about affiliation with this group?

What sort of customs do you practice that come from your racial/ethnic heritage?

Did you ever feel different from other people around you?

How would you describe your family's attitudes toward religion?

PERSONAL COPING WITHIN THIS SOCIAL ENVIRONMENT

- As a child and adolescent, how did the client perceive self within the family?
- What does the client like about him- or herself as a child? Dislike?
- As a child and adolescent, how did the client perceive each parent? As a child and adolescent, how did the client perceive roles of siblings?
- As a child and adolescent, how did the client perceive parents' regard for him or her?
- Ask the client to give three adjectives for each family member that describes how the client saw that person while the client was growing up.
- To what did client attribute academic success or failure?
- Did you ever imagine you were someone else? Somewhere else?

- What made you angry as a child? Frightened?
- Who could you go to for advice?
- What was your deepest secret?
- Were you ever embarrassed by anyone in your family? Describe.

Sample questions:
How did your family life prepare you to cope with life's challenges?
When something happened in the family to upset you, what did you do about it?
Did you ever feel alone or unloved?
Did you ever wish you would die?

FORMAL SYSTEMS INVOLVEMENT

Describe when and what type of services any member of the family received from these organizations:

- Public assistance (AFDC, TANF, Food Stamps)
- Emergency assistance (e.g., from private agency for food, shelter, clothing, payment of utility bill)
- Child welfare (protective services, foster care, adoption)
- Mental health clinic or provider
- Health care provider, hospital, or public health department
- Disabilities or special needs program
- Victim services program
- Family court for reasons other than delinquency (e.g., child support, adoption)
- Youth development program (e.g., Girls/Boys Clubs, sports club, summer camp)
- Law enforcement (list dates and type of incident, disposition)
- Juvenile justice agency
- Criminal justice system
- Military
- Drug or alcohol treatment program

Sample questions:
Did your family ever receive economic assistance (welfare)?
When your mother was depressed, did she receive services from a mental health provider? Do you recall which organization or place was the provider?
Did anyone in your family ever go to court for any reason?

ADULTHOOD

SOCIAL RELATIONS

- Client's residences since age 18, including location, type of dwelling, and who lived in the household
- Key friends and coworkers
- Describe any caregiving done by the client (e.g., babysitting, care of elderly relative)
- Affiliations such as leagues, clubs, online networks

Sample questions:
Who are the most important people in your life? Describe how you relate to her (him).
Would you say you form friendships easily?

INTIMATE RELATIONSHIPS

- List intimate partners and for each: nature of relationship; what was it about the partner that was attractive for the client; if separated or terminated relationship, reason
- If married or in a committed relationship, describe the history of the relationship and current dynamics
- What is the client's sexual identity?
- History of sexual behavior
- History of pregnancies, miscarriages, abortions

Sample questions:
What role does sexual intimacy play in your life?
What principles guide your sexual behavior?
In your current relationship, would you say that you are happy?
Think of the time when you separated from _____ [name]. Talk about how the decision to end the relationship happened.

FAMILY RELATIONS

- List the names and ages of the client's children, parents of each
- Describe dynamics of parent-child relations (client as parent), including children with whom the client lives, those who are in the custody of someone else, and adult children
- Describe the client's relationships with extended family

Sample questions:
Describe your philosophy as a parent.
Tell me about _____ *[name of client's child]*
What did you learn from your parent(s) about how to live in a family?

EMPLOYMENT/EDUCATION

- Client's vocational aspirations
- Highest job certification or educational level attained (e.g., GED?)
- List all jobs held: include employer, type of job, dates of employment, reason for leaving, salary level
- Describe work habits
- Quality of relations at work
- If there are periods of unemployment, why?
- How does the client perceive his or her job?
- If retired, how does the client feel about not working?

Sample questions:
Tell me about your work.
Are you satisfied with your current income level?

MILITARY SERVICE

- Reasons for enlisting; reasons for leaving
- Summary of assignments, any unusual circumstances
- Client's regard for jobs done in the service

Sample question:
What was it like in the military?

CONTRIBUTIONS TO COMMUNITY

- Community service
- Creative expression through music, art, drama, other
- Political involvement

Sample questions:
How would you describe yourself as a citizen of your community?
Do you regard yourself as a creative person? How do you express your creativity?
What do you do with your imagination?

DAILY LIVING

- Routine
- Health habits, hygiene
- Diet, exercise
- Sexual activity
- Recreation
- Hobbies
- Religious activity
- Civic participation

Sample questions:
What is a typical day in your life?
What are your main sources of contentment?
What are your main sources of stress?

SPIRITUALITY AND RELIGION

- Describe the client's religious practices
- Describe the role spirituality plays in the client's life

Sample questions:
Is spirituality an influence on your life? In what way?
How do your religious beliefs affect how you live your life?

ALCOHOL OR OTHER DRUG ABUSE

- Type of alcohol or drug use and age of onset
- Extent (e.g., amount, frequency of use)
- Symptoms of use (e.g., blackouts, withdrawal)
- Treatment (give type, dates, location)

Sample questions:
Have you ever used alcohol to the point of drunkenness? Passing out?
About how many drinks do you have each day? What kind?
What kind of drugs have you tried?
When you use [name drug mentioned by client], how does it make you feel? How often have you used _____ in the past month?

MENTAL HEALTH

- Worries, anxiety, depression
- Any perceptual problems (e.g., hallucinations, seeing things become larger or smaller or with an aura)

- Unexplained feelings (e.g., persecution, déjà vu, delusions)
- Describe any mental health treatment received
- Help-seeking behavior

Sample questions:
When you heard the voices, what did you do?
Who can you turn to in times of need?

HEALTH

- Health condition, illnesses, injuries (head injuries in particular), health care, medications
- Wellness practices; for example, nutrition, exercise, rest

Sample questions:
Have you ever been sick? What was the illness?

CRIMINAL ACTIVITY

- Arrests, convictions, sentences, probationary activities

Sample question:
Have you ever been in trouble with the law?

SELF-PERCEPTIONS

- How does the client regard self?
- How does the client reflect on his or her life?
- Overall, what does the client regard as high points? Low points?
- What have been the most important social relationships in the client's life?
- Vision of the future

Sample questions:
When you look back over your life, what do you see?
How have you changed over time?
What has been your greatest satisfaction in life? Your worst disap-
pointment?
What, if anything, would you change about your life?
What are your hopes for the future?

CLOSURE

- Encourage the client to offer any information about topics that may have been left out
- Discuss the client's feeling about the interview process

OBSERVATIONS

For each person interviewed, note:

- Consistency in disclosure of information
- Appearance
- Behavior; for example, movement, eye contact, activity, facial expressions
- Orientation in time and place
- Attention span
- Perception
- Memory
- Affect and mood
- Judgment
- Speech
- Indications of delusions, hallucinations, or suicidal ideation

Sample Family Social History Assessment Instruments

As noted in Chapter 4, many standardized checklists and inventories have been developed to guide gathering information and summarizing key facts and events, which are particularly helpful to the descriptive portion of a social history assessment. Some of these tools have been developed for research as well as clinical purposes. This list is not comprehensive—many other fine instruments are on the market. The following were selected for illustration.

Family Assessment Form: A Practice-Based Approach to Assessing Family Functioning

Source: Child Welfare League of America (http://www.cwla.org)

The Family Assessment Form (FAF) helps child welfare workers assess families, develop individualized family service plans, monitor progress, and assess outcomes. The FAF gives practitioners a structured way to document a psychosocial assessment by collecting information in six areas of family functioning: living conditions, financial conditions, social support, caregiver/child interactions, developmental stimulation, and caregiver interactions. Items on the FAF are rated on a 9-point scale (1, 1.5, 2, 2.5, etc.) in relation to family strengths and severity of concerns. A rating of 1 represents unusual strengths while a rating of 5 represents severe problems that may endanger a child's health and safety, threaten a caregiver's well-being, indicate severely dysfunctional family interactions, or call for removal of children from the family home. Workers are given the option to rate at the midway point between two numbers (i.e., 2.5 is between 2 and 3). Two additional areas are used for assessment purposes only: caregiver history and caregiver personal characteristics. Used during the initial assessment and then for periodic update assessments and at termination of services, the FAF tracks and identifies areas of continued concern and improvements in family functioning. The FAF software expedites assessment, facilitates service planning, documents casework, gathers and analyzes data, and runs reports on program activity and client outcomes.

Family Background Questionnaire (FBQ)

T. P. Melchert & T. V. Sayger

Source: Touliatos, J., Perlmutter, B. F., Straus, M. A., & Holden, G. W. (2000). *Handbook of Family Measurement Techniques* (Vol. 3). Thousand Oaks, CA: Sage.

The Family Background Questionnaire (FBQ) is a 179-item, 22-subscale questionnaire designed to assess adults' perceptions of their family of origin. Individual subscales focus on perceptions of either the subject's mother or father and measure the following variables: parental responsiveness, acceptance, physical and sexual abuse, expression of affect, physical neglect, parent involvement in education, decision-making style, control, chores, parental psychological adjustment, substance abuse, parental coalition, child social support, and family stressors. The full scale and subscales are scored by adding scores on individual items, after first reverse scoring half the items. Higher scores indicate higher levels of family functioning. The instrument was developed with a diverse sample of college students ($N = 676$) ranging in age from 18 to 72. The sample included 22% minorities. Four studies evaluating reliability and validity indicated high internal consistency estimates as measured by alpha, ranging from .76

to .96 (Melchert & Sayger, 1998). Test-retest correlations over a 2-week testing period ranged from .59 to .93 (Melchert & Sayger, 1998).

Additional References:

Melchert, T. P. (1998). Testing the validity of an instrument for assessing family of origin history. *Journal of Clinical Psychology, 54,* 863–875.

Melchert, T. P., & Sayger, T. V. (1998). The development of an instrument for measuring memories of family of origin characteristics. *Educational and Psychological Measurement, 58,* 99–118.

Family Connections Family Assessment

Source: University of Maryland-Baltimore Family Connections Project

http://www.family.umaryland.edu/research/outline.pdf

The Family Connections Family Assessment includes a social history component that assesses the social history of the family of origin and addresses attachment, nurturance, stability, deprivation or maltreatment, and overall development. This section identifies the critical life incidents (positive and stressful) and describes the relationships of the family members (including sexual history). This measure has been used in research projects conducted at the University of Maryland-Baltimore Family Connections Project. The author of this index could not find any published research that provided information regarding reliability, validity, or use of this measure with diverse populations.

Family Inventory of Life Events and Changes (FILE)

Source: McCubbin, H. I., & Patterson, J. M. (1987). FILE: Family Inventory of Life Events and Changes. In H. I. McCubbin & A. I. Thompson (Eds.), *Family assessment inventories for research and practice* (pp. 81–98). Madison: University of Wisconsin–Madison, Family Stress Coping and Health Project.

Based on family systems theory and family stress theory, the Family Inventory of Life Events and Changes (FILE) is a 71-item self-report instrument designed to record normative and nonnormative life events and changes experienced by the whole family unit in the past 12 months. Using a *yes-no* response format, adult family members are asked to respond by checking whether or not each event listed occurred within the past year. Events are grouped into nine categories: intrafamily strains, marital strains, pregnancy and childbearing strains, finance and business strains, work-family transitions and strains, illness and family "care" strains, losses, transitions "in" and "out," and legal; although more current research (Barton & Baglio, 1993) suggests a 10-subscale structure that includes "Trouble With Teenagers."

The manual is well organized and easy to use. National norms are available, based on approximately 980 couples (1,960 individuals), including couples across the family life cycle. FILE can be scored in five ways, depending on the purpose and ultimate use of the information. The five types of scores are (1) family life events score, (2) family-couple life events score, (3) family-couple discrepancy score, (4) family readjustment score, and (5) family-couple readjustment score. Although the FILE is easy to administer and score, one must be aware that all items are weighted equally in one of the scoring formats (i.e., family life events score), assuming that each one has equal import to the respondent. Weighted scores are provided for the readjustment scores to reflect the relative "stressfulness" of items. For the family life events score, an overall sum score is calculated, with higher scores implying lower stress. Reliability and validity information is available in the manual, with overall scale reliability ranging from .72 to .81. Pearson r for test-retest reliability over a 4- to 5-week period ranged from .66 to .84. Concurrent validity was examined through the comparison of the FILE to the Moos Family Environment Scale (FES). Correlations between the FILE and the Moos FES ranged from −.24 to +.23 on the total scale score. The author of this index found no specific information regarding use with diverse populations.

Additional References:

Barton, K., & Baglio, C. (1993). The nature of stress in child-abusing families: A factor analytic study. *Psychological Reports, 73*(3, Pt. 1), pp. 1047–1055.

Patterson, J. M. (1985). Critical factors affecting family compliance with home treatment for children with cystic fibrosis. *Family Relations, 34,* 79–89.

Patterson, J. M., & McCubbin, H. I. (1983). The impact of family life events and changes on the health of a chronically ill child. *Family Relations, 32,* 255–264.

Plummer, L. P., & Koch-Hattem, A. (1986). Family stress and adjustment to divorce. *Family Relations, 35,* 523–529.

Family Inventory of Life Events and Changes (FILE)—Adolescent Version

Source: McCubbin, H. I., Patterson, J. M., & Harris, L. H. (2000). Adolescent Family Inventory of Life Events and Changes [1991]. In K. Corcoran & J. Fisher, *Measures for clinical practice: A sourcebook* (3rd ed., Vol. 1, pp. 197–203). New York: Free Press.

This 50-item self-report records life events and changes that adolescents perceive their families to have experienced during the past 12 months. It also records life events occurring prior to the period and that require longer periods to adapt to. The Family Inventory of Life Events and Changes (FILE)—Adolescent Version (A-FILE) is used for research and counseling to assess the stress an adolescent may be experiencing as a result of an accrual of life events and changes occurring in the family. An index of family vulnerability to change is made and adolescents are identified who are at risk of experiencing undesirable outcomes. Norms are available and this measure is commonly used in research. A-FILE is available in print and microfiche.

Family of Origin Recollections (FOR)

Source: Lewis, J. M., & Owen, M. T. (1995). Stability and change in family-of-origin recollections over the first four years of parenthood. *Family Process, 34,* 455–469.

The Family of Origin Recollections (FOR) is a 20-item Likert-type questionnaire to evaluate adults' perceptions of their parents and their parents' marriage during their childhood and adolescence. Various Likert-type response formats are used, including 4-, 5-, and 6-point scales. Items were adapted from Shareshefsky and Yarrow's (1973) interviews with adults regarding family-of-origin perceptions during their childhood and adolescence. The FOR is not generally treated as a composite scale; instead each item is individually interpreted and compared. A measure of test-retest reliability over a 4.5 year period using a sample of both men and women ($N = 56$) indicated a correlation of .50 or above for most items.

Additional References:

Shareshefsky, P. M., & Yarrow, L. J. (1973). *Psychological aspects of a first pregnancy and early postnatal adaptation.* New York: Raven.
Touliatos, J., Perlmutter, B. F., Straus, M. A., & Holden, G. W. (2000). *Handbook of family measurement techniques* (Vol. 2, pp. 54–55). Thousand Oaks, CA: Sage.

Family Social History Questionnaire

Source: Nurturing Parenting Programs, http://www.nurturingparenting.com

The Family Social History Questionnaire is a self-report inventory given pre- and posttest to gather information regarding the family demographics (age, gender, income, education level, etc.) and perceptions of childhood history. Participants rate the quality of their life with their partners and children. Each complete Nurturing Parenting Program comes with a package of 40 Family Social History Questionnaires. The author of this index could not find any published research that provided information regarding reliability, validity, or use of this measure with diverse populations.

Multigenerational Interconnectedness Scales (MIS)

Source: Gavazzi, S. M., Sabatelli, R. M., & Reese-Weber, M. J. (1999). Measurement of the financial, functional, and psychological connections in families: Conceptual development and empirical use of the Multigenerational Interconnectedness Scale. *Psychological Reports, 84,* 1361–1371. E-mail: gavazzi.1@osu.edu

The Multigenerational Interconnectedness Scales (MIS) is a 31-item Likert-type, self-report questionnaire designed to assess connectedness of late adolescents and young adults with their family of origin. Three specific areas of connectedness assessed are financial (8 items), functional (8 items), and psychological (15 items). Financial interconnectedness refers to the extent to which adolescents or young adults rely on their family of origin for help in paying bills or obtaining material resources. Functional interconnectedness refers to the extent to which adolescents or young adults share in daily activities with their family of origin. Finally, psychological interconnectedness refers to emotional dependence on one's family of origin. Items are on a 7-point scale and scores are computed for the three subscales listed above and an overall score by summing and/or averaging responses. Higher scores indicated greater connectedness. A factor analysis of this instrument indicated that all items loaded .30 or above. Measures of internal consistency reliability indicated a correlation of .86 for the financial subscale, .82 for functional, .84 for psychological, and .87 for the overall score. MIS scores were negatively correlated with age, with age being more related to connectedness for females than for males.

Additional References:

Bartle, S. E. (1993). The degree of similarity of differentiation of self between partners in married and dating couples: Preliminary evidence. *Contemporary Family Therapy, 15,* 467–484.

Bartle, S. E., Anderson, S. A., & Sabatelli, R. M. (1989). A model of parenting style, adolescent individuation, and adolescent self-esteem. *Journal of Adolescent Research, 4,* 283–298.

Gavazzi, S. M., & Sabatelli, R. M. (1990). Family system dynamics, the individuation process, and psychological development. *Journal of Adolescent Research, 5,* 500–519.

Person-in-Environment (PIE)

J. M. Karls & K. E. Wandrei

Source: CompuPIE (http://www.compupie.org)

Person-in-Environment (PIE), developed for social workers, identifies and classifies problems in social functioning according to four factors:

1. Social relationships (family, interpersonal, occupational, special life situations; type problem; severity and duration; capacity to solve the problem)

2. Environment (resources for basic needs such as food, housing, economic resources, transportation; education and training; judicial and legal system; health, welfare, and safety resources; nonprofit and faith sector involvement; helping networks)

3. Mental health needs according to *DSM-IV*

4. Physical health problems as diagnosed by a physician or reported by the client

The PIE system produces a standardized report of assessment findings and recommended interventions.

Quickview Social History

Ronald A. Gianetti, PhD

Source: Pearson Assessments (http://www.pearsonassessments.com)

The Quickview Social History is an inventory of questions that enables the interviewer to collect a standardized set of social and clinical data in a minimal amount of time. It may be administered by paper and pencil or computer. Designed for used with clients age 16 and over, the inventory captures information about social, psychological, and physical conditions and is designed to facilitate diagnoses in the *DSM-IV* (*Diagnostic and Statistical Manual;* American Psychiatric Association, 1994). The history covers nine areas: demographics and identifying information, developmental history, family of origin, educational history, marital history, occupational history/financial status, legal history, military history, and symptom screen (psychological and physical). The inventory includes 235 items and takes 30–45 minutes to complete. The program produces a descriptive narrative report and offers suggestions for follow-up interview questions. A sample report is available on the Web site.

Social Environment Inventory (SEI)

Source: Orr, S. T., James, S. A., & Charney, E. (1989). A social environment inventory for the pediatric office. *Developmental and Behavioral Pediatrics, 10,* 287–291.

The Social Environment Inventory (SEI) is a 35-item self-report instrument designed to record the presence of specific stressful situations experienced in the past 12 months by a family that has preschool/elementary age children. Using a *yes-no* format, mothers are asked to respond by checking whether or not each event/experience listed occurred in the past year. Events are categorized as follows: dimensions of marital relationships, family health, employment, housing, finances, children, schools, parents, and crime/legal issues. The questionnaire does not contain division among items, and the total score simply reflects the total number of stressors to which the mother answered "yes." The SEI has been used primarily with mothers who brought their children to see pediatricians in the Baltimore area. The scale was developed using diverse samples and test-retest reliability estimates ($N = 141$) over a period of 30 days were .74. Criterion validity was assessed comparing the SEI to a measure of depression. Elevated depression scores were 3.65 times more prevalent among women in the highest SEI group.

Additional Version:

Prenatal Social Environment Inventory (PSEI)

Source: Orr, S. T., James, S. A., & Casper, R. (1992). Psychosocial stressors and low birth weight: Development of a questionnaire. *Journal of Developmental and Behavioral Pediatrics, 13*(5), 343–347.

The Prenatal Social Environment Inventory (PSEI) was designed to assess exposure to stressors among pregnant women. This 41-item scale was developed using interview data from 244 women selected from obstetric practices. Reliability and validity of the PSEI were assessed with 221 obstetric patients. The PSEI had test-retest and internal consistency correlations of .73 and .80, respectively. An analysis conducted to examine concurrent validity indicated that the PSEI significantly and positively correlated with scores on the Center for Epidemiologic Studies Depression Scale. Based on these results, the PSEI appears to be a reliable and valid measure for assessing exposure to stressors among pregnant women in clinical settings.

Checklist for Social History Records Compilation

When possible, a thorough history assessment includes a review of recorded facts about the life. Such records describe and establish dates for life milestones and critical events while introducing the cast of characters in the person's life. Written records, while subject to occasional inaccuracies, are generally filed by various professionals and are reliable. They serve to legitimize narrative reports from interviewees. Sometimes critical information about the person's life circumstances is in the records of a family member other than the person, such as a mother's medical records. Obviously, permission from the subject of the record will be required to obtain copies of most records. In many cases, substantial time is required for bureaucratic organizations to locate and copy the records.

List of Social History Records

1. Health records
   a. Birth certificate (in some states, public health departments gather background information at birth that is part of a central record but not part of the birth certificate or medical record; this detailed information about such factors as mother and infant's health conditions can be particularly helpful)
   b. Health care records from physicians, clinics, hospitals
   c. Death certificates

2. Family and individual social service records, such as
   a. Marriage, separation, divorce, and child support records (at Family Court, marriage and divorce published in newspaper)
   b. Child welfare records (protective services, foster care, adoption; these records often include placement and discharge reports,

progress reports, and evaluations of the child's health, mental health, and educational status)

    c. Economic assistance participation (Food Stamps, AFDC or TANF, WIC (Special Supplemental Nutrition Program for Women, Infants, and Children)

    d. Emergency assistance (generally these are private sector agencies) for shelter, food, or clothing

    e. Housing assistance through public or nonprofit agency programs

3. School records

    a. For each grade: child's address, transcripts, standardized test scores, special education testing or classes, intelligence evaluations, support services participation (e.g., counseling or school-based mental health), discipline record, GED, adult education

4. Psychological and psychiatric records

    a. From clinics, private providers, residential treatment programs and hospitals, alcohol and other drug abuse treatment programs (records would include patient's address, evaluations, treatment, progress, medication logs, and discharge reports)

5. Youth development programs

    a. Records of participation in after-school programs, summer camps, Boys/Girls Clubs or other structured activities, sports clubs, community service

6. Faith community record

    a. Record of church, synagogue, mosque, or other faith community membership

    b. Certificate of baptism or confirmation

7. Juvenile justice records, including

    a. Defense counsel's records

    b. Community service records

    c. Juvenile detention records, evaluation records, treatment plans, progress notes, discharge plans

    d. Court files

8. Employment records, including

    a. Applications, job assignments, and performance evaluations

    b. On-the-job medical and psychological evaluations

    c. Time records

    d. Relocations

    e. Workers' compensation records

    f. Pay records, Social Security tax records

9. Military service records, including

    a. Enlistment and discharge orders

    b. Record of service assignments

    c. Record of honors and disciplinary actions

10. Criminal records, including

    a. Rap sheets

    b. Court records

    c. Defense counsel and prosecution files

    d. Local police, sheriff, and FBI records

    e. Jail and prison records, to include health, mental health, or educational assessments and interventions in criminal justice settings; progress notes and disciplinary reports; work assignments; classification reports; participation in vocational, educational, religious, and honor programs; visitation logs

    f. Probation and parole records, including pre-sentence investigation and sentencing reports; probation officer records and notes; conditions of supervision; violations; conditions of release from supervision

11. Civil litigation records, such as

    a. Bankruptcy

    b. Insurance claims

    c. Lawsuits

12. Immigration and Naturalization Service (INS)/U.S. Citizenship and Immigration Services (USCIS) records (e.g., applications, hearing transcripts, findings, orders, and reports)

13. Media reports about the subject or anyone in the subject's family (e.g., sports participation, accidents, crime reports)

14. Family records

    a. Photo albums or collections, scrapbooks, journals

    b. Wills, deeds, titles

Record Sources

1. Federal sources

    a. The National Archives and Records Administration (NARA)

The federal government permits opening of census records 72 years after the record is made. These records contain names, ages, income, location, and other information about household members who were recorded in the census.
(http://www.nara.gov/genealogy/genindex.html)

b. U.S. Bureau of the Census
The place for links to community profiles.
(http://www.census/gov/)

c. Social Security Administration
The SSA maintains detailed earnings records of anyone who was employed and paid into the Social Security system. This information helps track location and socioeconomic status of people in a social network.
(http://www.ssa.gov/mystatement/)

d. National Personnel Record Center, St. Louis, MO
This office maintains records of everyone who has served in the U.S. military:
(http://www.archives.gov/st-louis/military-personnel/index .html)

e. Library of Congress, Local History and Genealogy Reading Room
(http://lcweb.loc.gov/rr/genealogy)

f. U.S. Department of Health and Human Services, National Center for Health Statistics, *Where to write for vital records.*
(http://www.cec.gov/nchs/howto/w2w/w2welcom/htm)

2. State sources

a. State health department vital records

These offices keep birth and death certificates. Birth records include information about birth location, infant health status (in some areas), parents and their residence. Death certificates likewise include location and cause of death, thus providing information for health histories.

b. State law enforcement and corrections

These records, which are typically maintained by name of the offender, not victim, include records of convicted criminals. The National Crime Information Center provides links to state criminal records offices.
(http://www.fbi.gov/hq/cjisd/ncic.htm)

c. Local records

Tracing records at local schools, hospitals, courts, social service agencies, police stations, jails, and other organizations can be time-consuming but often fruitful in that these records tend to contain more detail than state or federal records. Many have social history reports in them.

3. Genealogy sources

a. The Family History Library of the Church of Jesus Christ of Latter-day Saints

(http://www.familysearch.org)

The Mormon Church has developed a vast repository of information from around the world about their church members and nonmembers.

b. National Genealogical Society (NGS)

(http://www.ngsgealogy.org)

The NGS is a nonprofit organization that provides education, information, publications, research assistance, and networking for people who are interested in searching their genealogies.

c. Genealogy.com is a Web-based business that offers extensive support and linkages to people who are searching their family histories. See http://www.genealogy.com and http://www.myfamily.com.

d. The USGenWeb Project, affiliated with the U.S. National Archives, is a group of volunteers who provide Internet Web sites for genealogical research in every county and in every state of the United States. This Project is noncommercial and fully committed to free access for everyone. (http://www.usgenweb.org)

4. International

Familysearch.org (above) provides a link to international online records and sources. Also, the U.S. Department of State provides a list of consulates for foreign countries where questions about links to international vital records may be directed. (http://www.state.gov/s/cpr/rls/fco/)

5. Cultural groups

This list, by no means exhaustive, is intended to illustrate sources of information about individuals from particular ethnic and cultural groups in the United States. The largest groups are mentioned here.

Immigration History Research Center—University of Minnesota
(http://www.umn.edu/ihrc/)

Statue of Liberty and Ellis Island Foundation, Inc.
(http://www.ellisisland.org)

Web sites for people of African ancestry
Afrigeneas (http://www.afrigeneas.com)
African American Genealogy Group (http://www.aagg.org/)

Native American genealogy links at these Web sites
(http://members.aol.com/bbbenge/front.html
http://www.native-languages.org/genealogy.htm)

Latin American genealogy links at these Web sites
(http://www.lasculturas.com/lib/libGenealogy.htm
http://genealogy.about.com/od/hispanic/)

Asian American genealogical links at this Web site
(http://www.cetel.org/)

People of Jewish ancestry
United States Holocaust Museum (http://www.ushmm.org)

Tools to Describe Social Relationships

The genogram (family tree) and sociogram (ecomap) are tools frequently used in development of a social history.

Genogram

Almost every thorough social history will include a genogram, or family tree, to map the family structure and relationships. With a few symbols, names, dates, and theme words, the family's basic functioning can be captured in a single picture. See discussion below of software by McGoldrick, Gerson, and Shellenberger (1999) and of a guidebook by DeMaria, Weeks, and Hof (1999). The term *family tree* should always be used instead of *genogram* with laypeople because family members and key reviewers such as jurors will understand it better. The genogram is a tool used during fact gathering (while interviewing family members) and in court, as evidence.

The basics are simple: Circles depict females, squares are males. Solid lines represent blood or legal relations, dotted lines are foster or voluntary relations. By arranging the symbols, the following aspects of the family composition emerge:

- Dates and identities for marriages, separations (single slash), or divorce (double slash)
- Dates and identities for pregnancies, spontaneous and induced abortions, births, adoptions, fostering of children
- Dates and identities of illness, injury, or death (cause in word)
- Birth order
- Ethnic, class, and/or religious identification (words)
- Occupation and/or educational level
- Significant characteristics or events associated with individuals (e.g., mental illness, alcohol or drug abuse, disease or disability, prodigy)
- Conflict or close bond in relationship

The genogram may include a legend that identifies the key themes. An image becomes associated with a theme, such as a bottle for alcohol abuse, the Greek letter *psi* for mental illness, a book for learning problem, or a dollar sign with a slash over it for economic poverty. The words to describe the themes should be nontechnical, such as "learning problem" instead of "cognitive deficit," and specific, such as "physical abuse," "violence," or "sexual abuse" instead of "child abuse." The themes are easier to follow when they are color coded (use no more than four colors or the figure will be too complicated to read).

The genogram should include all people who were closely involved in the person's life; none should be selectively excluded. Those that had a relatively minor role in the life can be portrayed with smaller circles or squares.

In the "Simple Genogram" (see Figure 6.1), the primary subject, depicted in a bold circle, is the daughter of two biological parents, one of whom is deceased due to heart disease. She has been married to one husband for 29 years, and they are the biological parents of two children and the adoptive parents of one child. The biological and adoptive daughters have a particularly close relationship. No obvious social or psychological problems are noted in this family except for propensity for heart disease.

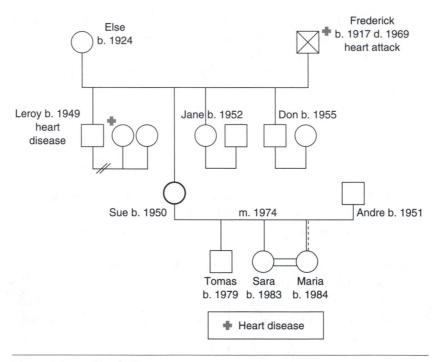

Figure 6.1   Simple Genogram

In its simplest form, the family tree can be quite elegant, as Figure 6.1 demonstrates.[1] In a more challenging case, the family has lived through chaos and multiple broken attachments, and the picture is anything but simple. The social historian will almost always draw a genogram for working purposes, to clarify the cast of characters and summarize themes. This genogram will be complex (see Figure 6.2).

The social history expert's key role is to interpret the patterns that appear as the family tree emerges. Observations about intergenerational traits, coincidences of dates, atypical relations, and repetitious behaviors or conflict patterns bring clarity to the confusion.

For example, the social historian is likely to make the following observations about the facts depicted in Figure 6.2, a complex family tree for Emma Blane, who entered a dissociative state and abandoned her grandchild (see the case history in Chapter 5).

- Ms. Blane is descended from two biological parents with personal histories of mental disturbance, as indicated by the *psi* symbol. Her mother, though undiagnosed by any formal systems, showed

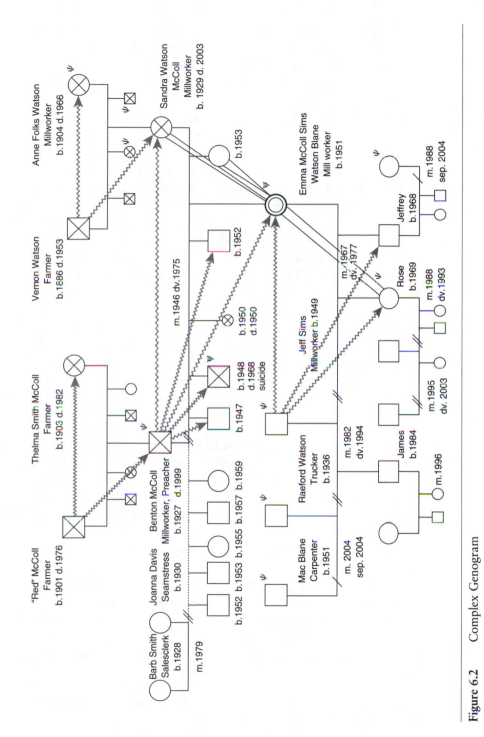

Figure 6.2   Complex Genogram

163

clear signs of major and persistent depression and dependent personality. Her father has numerous antisocial symptoms. Her brother committed suicide, her oldest son married a woman with serious mental illness, and her daughter has major depression. Her husbands all have antisocial traits.

- Emma's biological father (Benton) was raised by a father who beat him and his mother, as indicated by the unidirectional arrows with conflict lines. Emma's biological mother also came from a home with an abusive father. The pattern of male violence was repeated by her father against his wife and children and also by her first husband Jeff.
- Benton and Sandra's marriage ended in divorce. Benton's relationship with his second family also ended with a break-up. Emma repeated this pattern of broken partnerships with her three husbands, as have her daughter Rose and son Jeffrey.
- Emma had a close relationship with her mother and has closeness with her sister and daughter, as indicated by the double lines.
- This drawing clearly demonstrates the intergenerational patterns of abuse, psychological disturbance, and gender differences. Notably, Emma's son Jeffrey has not engaged in violence but instead chose a highly dependent wife, one who has a chronic mental illness. She left him against his will, leaving the children in his care.

When discussing the genogram with family members or other professionals, its complexity can be simplified by color coding, introducing sections at a time (phasing in the presentation), minimizing minor figures, or using only those portions of the tree that illustrate the key points raised by the discussion. Family members who provide information for the genogram often find the drawing to be enlightening and helpful to their own understanding of their family situation.

Without a genogram, the person's story can be difficult to follow as the cast of characters and their complex relationships to one another are narrated. With a genogram as a backdrop, the story line becomes easier to follow. The professional and the person who is the subject of the history are likely to refer to the genogram repeatedly as the story unfolds, pointing to figures as their part in the history is told.

The following are two excellent resources for instructions on how to create genograms:

McGoldrick, M., Gerson, R., & Shellenberger, S. (1999). *Genograms: Assessment and intervention* (2nd ed.). New York: Norton.

Synopsis: McGoldrick, Gerson, and Shellenberger (1999) provide a standardized format, software (GenoWare™ in 1999, since updated to GenoPro™), and interpretive principles on which genograms are based. Genograms can be completed in one or two interview sessions. The authors suggest an outline for the interview that includes gathering information from the family of origin on both sides of the family, ethnicity, major moves, significant others, and other information such as serious medical, behavioral, or emotional problems; job problems; drug or alcohol problems; spirituality, and so on. Some research has shown that clinicians who use a genogram are considerably more accurate in recording names of family members and somewhat more accurate at recording unnamed persons, relationships, and medical issues (Coupland, Serovich, & Glenn, 1995). Additional research has indicated low agreement in what sections of the genogram clinicians identify as most important, and some research has argued that the clinical use of genograms is still not well understood (Rohrbaugh, Rogers, & McGoldrick, 1992). Guidelines for interpretation of genograms can be found in McGoldrick et al. (1999).

DeMaria, R., Weeks, G., & Hof, L. (1999). *Focused genograms: Intergenerational assessment of individuals, couples, and families.* Philadelphia, PA: Brunner/ Mazel.

Synopsis: Genograms are often used to plot a focused theme in a family's history, such as spirituality, culture, or a specific concern (e.g., addiction, infertility, disability). DeMaria, Weeks, and Hof (1999) offer numerous examples of focused genograms. The authors encourage using standard symbols on genograms and creatively adapting the content to meet the need of the family or client.

Additional references about genograms include the following:

Coupland, S., Serovich, J., & Glenn, J. (1995). Reliability in constructing genograms: A study among marriage and family therapy doctoral students. *Journal of Marital and Family Therapy, 21*(3), 251–263.

Cox, R. P., Keltner, N., & Hogan, B. (2003). Family assessment tools. In R. P. Cox (Ed.), *Health related counseling with families of diverse cultures: Family, health, and cultural competencies* (pp. 145–167). Westport, CT: Greenwood.

Erdman, H. P., & Foster, S. W. (1986). Computer-assisted assessment with couples and families. *Family Therapy, 13*(1), 23–40.

Rigazio-DiGilio, S. A., Ivey, A. E., & Kunkler-Peck, K. P. (2005). *Community genograms: Using individual, family, and cultural narratives with clients.* New York: Teachers College Press.

Rohrbaugh, M., Rogers, J., & McGoldrick, M. (1992). How do experts read family genograms? *Family Systems Medicine, 10*(1), 79–89.

Timm, T., & Blow, A. (2005). The family life cycle and the genogram. In M. Cierpka, T. Volker, & D. H. Sprenkle (Eds.), *Family assessment: Integrating multiple perspectives* (pp. 159–191). Ashland, OR: Hogrefe & Huber.

Watts, C., & Shrader, E. (1998). The genogram: A new research tool to document patterns of decision-making, conflict and vulnerability within households. *Health Policy Planning, 13*(4), 459–464.

Sociogram or Ecomap

A sociogram (also known as an ecomap) helps describe qualities of social relationships within a cultural context (Hartman, 1995). Sociograms, used occasionally in social history assessment, are particularly useful when the dynamics of the person's social circle or cultural status (such as minority or immigrant status within a specific community) are essential to understanding the person. The sociogram can be useful during fact gathering as the person and others in the social network describe their relations to one another

Sociograms have become popular tools in many settings, such as organizations that are training teams to work together or interorganizational community coalitions that collaborate for a common goal. Whatever their purpose, sociograms have two essential features: (1) depiction of key players in the social network with indications of the type of relationships among them and (2) depiction of relevant factors in the external environment of the social network. The primary figure is in the center, surrounded by individuals or groups with whom some sort of social relation could exist. The types of relationships are symbolized by different lines to depict nurture, tension, abuse, exchange, and other dynamics.

The person who draws the sociogram can freely design the appropriate symbols to suit the specific types of relationships in the system and will develop a key for the specific types of relationships involved. Generally, circles depict individuals or groups (including organizations). Relative size of the circles indicates their significance to the social system. Proximity of circles to one another indicates closeness of the individuals or groups to one another. Lines of various sizes and shapes symbolize the nature of the relationships between circles.

Figure 6.3 illustrates a case that involved an African American man, Thomas, who was born and raised in a segregated southern U.S. community. An explanation of its elements follows.

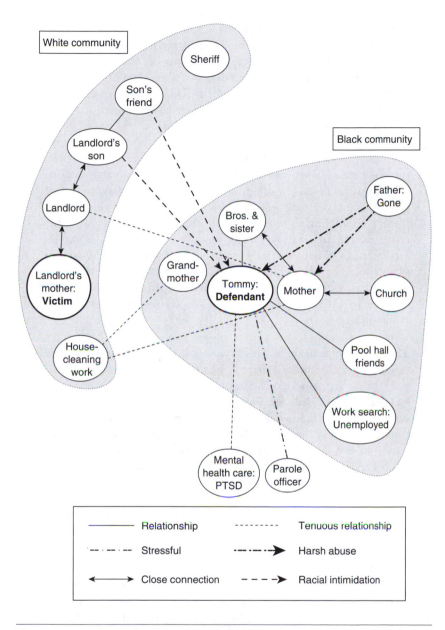

Figure 6.3   Sociogram (Ecomap): Example From a Racially Segregated
Rural Southern U.S. Community

Note: This sociogram is drawn with Microsoft Word 2000.

The separation of the Black and White communities is symbolized by the dotted lines that surround those considered inside each—the only connections between people in each community are tenuous or hostile. Two figures, the mental health center and the parole officer, serve the community but are located outside it. Thomas was convicted of killing an elderly white female neighbor; he fatally injured her while attempting to rob her home. A high school dropout, the young defendant (Thomas) was on parole after serving time for larceny. Thomas had difficulty holding a job, partly because the unemployment rate for Black males in his community was over 20%, and partly because he had serious mental health problems. He had been diagnosed with posttraumatic stress disorder while in high school subsequent to his father's attempting to beat him to death. The public mental health center agreed to treat him with sessions twice a month, but the facility was a twenty-five mile ride from his mother's house, and he often could not get a ride. Thomas's mother, an active member of her church, worked as a domestic housekeeper and lived with her children in a former sharecropper's old frame house on a white family's farm.

The relationships between African American and White women in the community were cordial, though tenuous, but those among men could get hostile. Twice, when Thomas was a teenager, local white boys, including the landlord's son, drove by the cabin with shotguns pointed out of the cars' windows. They shot at Thomas and the other African American boys in the yard, yelling "Dance, nigger!" Thomas and his family never called law enforcement because in their community, they did not trust the white sheriff to help on such matters.

The victim was the grandmother of the landlord's son. Thomas had no direct relation with the victim prior to the time of the crime, although their social networks were connected.

Sociograms show the vitality of a family within its larger ecosystem, revealing exchanges and blockages of energy. Sociograms can illustrate active relationships; they can also depict what is missing, such as the absence of key resources, or problems in a relationship that should be based on nurture and exchange. For example, the professional might discuss essential social supports, such as consistent care, positive peer relations, experience demonstrating competence in community settings, and others. An example in one case would be church, scouts, sports team, and neighborhood friends. If it is revealed that these relationships were broken or blocked, as each is discussed with the person, the professional could cross the figure out, denoting absence or loss of the essential resource. The process of constructing the figure, not just the end product, promotes understanding of the family structure and functioning.

Tools to Describe Life Events

Most often, a social history is presented in chronological order. Humans tend to think in terms of time, particularly when they examine history. Thus the social historian must devise ways to present the facts in a life history in comprehensible chronological order. When based on the chronology, the life history calendar is a tool that helps to summarize key themes in the chronology. And, in the briefest manner, based on the life history calendar, the major relevant facts may be drawn on a time line.

Chronology

The chronology is the core background tool for organizing facts that are gathered through the social history records and interviews. The format is simple: two columns, a narrow one for dates and a wide one for recording the facts. The dates are as specific as possible, including time of day when relevant, and are in chronological order. The facts are always followed by notation regarding the source(s) of the information. An excerpt was included in Chapter 4.

Information is logged onto the chronology when it has been gathered and determined by the professional to be reliable. Information of questionable accuracy or validity can be included but should be marked as questionable. Sometimes various family members give contradictory information or recall events in different sequences. This can be included with special notation regarding the sources and inconsistencies.

The following excerpt from a chronology illustrates the detail that is entered into the chronology. All documents to support the chronology, including interview notes and records, should be filed for easy retrieval in case the original sources need to be consulted.

Excerpt From Life Chronology

1966   prenatal period

Jan.   Frieda Reagan, Toby's mother, worked for Sampson Industries and earned $121.55 between January and March. [Social Security Administration Itemized Statement of Earnings]

3-6   Frieda Reagan was admitted to Lughaven Hospital for a bullet wound in the left leg. The family address was listed as Route 1, Round O, Alabama, and Tobias's employer was listed as Rhodes Furniture and Frieda as a housewife. The records list Frieda's past medical history as being treated by Dr. Smith for nervousness. Reason for bullet wound was reported by patient to be accidental. [Lughaven Hospital Records] Frieda now says her husband Tobias shot her. [ABA interview with Frieda Hanson 8-19-1999]

3-9   Frieda Reagan was discharged from the hospital with the final diagnosis listed as gunshot wound to the left leg. The wound was cleaned and dressed. [Lughaven Hospital Records]

c. 1966 Frieda Reagan had a kidney infection and was medicated during the pregnancy for Toby (defendant). There are no medical records because the doctor and the practice are no longer around. [ABA Interview of Frieda Reagan Hansen 7-14-06]

1967   birth year

4-7   Frieda Reagan, Toby's mother, was admitted to Lughaven Hospital at 7:40 p.m. for "term pregnancy." The family was living at Route 1, Round O, Alabama, in Jefferson County. Tobias Reagan's employer was listed as Rhodes Furniture. The doctor was listed as Dr. Smith. [Lughaven Hospital Records]

4-8   Toby was born at 1:30 a.m. at Lughaven Memorial hospital and weighed 6 pounds 11 ounces. He was delivered by Dr. Smith. The records show that the baby was "apparently normal." From the time Frieda found out she was pregnant with Toby, Tobias thought that it was not his child. He told Frieda this every day and said he would not raise a bastard. Frieda tried to assure him that this was his child; however she doesn't think Tobias ever believed it. She told Tobias that if it was not his child she would "get rid of it." However, Tobias said that if anything happened to the child that would just prove it was not his. Frieda says at times it was so stressful that she wished she was not pregnant. She would lift things that were too heavy, such as wash tubs full of water, wishing to end the pregnancy. But then she feared Tobias would beat her because that would prove it was not his child. Frieda did not take care of herself and did not take the appropriate vitamins.

She continued to smoke and drink coffee. Frieda stated that Tobias Reagan continued to abuse her physically throughout the pregnancy. Frieda stated that the delivery took too long so Tobias left her alone at the hospital and he was not present for the birth. [Birth Certificate, ABA and KP Interview of Frieda Hansen 8-19-06, 8-26-06 and 10-2-06, and Lughaven Hospital Records]

4-10   Frieda Reagan was discharged from the hospital after the live birth of her son Tobias James Reagan, Jr. [Lughaven Hospital Records]

c. Nov.   Toby crawled at 7 months. [Shared Services Special Education Home Study]

1968   age 1

April   Toby walked at 1 year. [Shared Services Special Education Home Study]

June   Toby toilet trained at 14 months. [Shared Services Special Education Home Study]

Life History Calendar

The life history calendar is a background tool to help the life historian clearly see critical events, chronic conditions, coinciding events, and missing information (Caspi et al., 1996). The tool, essentially a grid, creates a comprehensive picture in a relatively short form. The calendar records long-term patterns of behavior and streams of events, transitions (specific or critical life events), and crises. The calendar identifies the timing, duration, and patterns of multiple life events, such as repetitive themes or escalating or declining trends. Both continuity and change can be measured.

In Figure 6.4, the sample calendar covers two years of a child's life. The patterns that emerge reveal instability (changing residences, schools, and mother's jobs), abuse (victim of sexual abuse and exposure to domestic violence), and psychological problems (sleep disturbance and bedwetting, probably subsequent to sexual abuse and violence exposure, and behavior problems at school). The continuing presence of the grandmother and mother indicate persistent attachments. The expert would note the tender age of the child at the time of these serious stressors. These two years would be considered in the context of the whole life, with a calendar for each year.

Figure 6.5 shows a different type of chart with the same information. This case requires more concise information year by year, so some detail is lost. These two models demonstrate the flexibility that historians have in presenting the information—the format should fit the need.

Figure 6.4 Excerpt From Life History Calendar (Model 1)

	1984												1985											
Year																								
Age	5		6										7											
	J	F	M	A	M	J	J	A	S	O	N	D	J	F	M	A	M	J	J	A	S	O	N	D
Residence/Household																								
At grandmom's	+	+	+	+	+	+	+	+						+	+	+	+	+	+	+	+	+	+	+
At mom's, live-in boyfriends									+	+	+	+	+											
Education																								
Church day care	+	+	+	+																				
CG Grinnell School									+	+	+	+	+								+	+		
RB Hayes School														+	+	+	+	+	+	+			+	+
Work																								
Mom: waitress, changing jobs	+	+				+	+	+	+	+	+	+	+	+	+	+	+	+	+	+	+	+	+	+
Key Relationships																								
Grandmom, mom	+	+	+	+	+	+	+	+	+	+	+	+	+	+	+	+	+	+	+	+	+	+	+	+
Key Events																								
Repeated fights at school												×	×								×	×	×	×
Crim Dom. Viol reports, boyfriend				×		×											×							
DSS founded case, sexual abuse																					×			
Custody to grandmom																								×
Sleep disturbance, bedwetting				×	×											×	×				×	×	×	×

Year	Age	Residence/ household	Education	Work	Key relationships	Key events
1984	5-6	Grandmom	Day care	Mom	Mom, grandmom	CDV
1985	6-7	Grandmom, mom	1st grade	Mom	Mom, grandmom	Sexual abuse
1986	7-8	Grandmom, mom	2 school–2nd grade	Mom	Mom, grandmom, fights w/peers	CDV, custody to grandmom, bedwetting

Figure 6.5   Excerpt From Life History Calendar (Model 2)

Time Line

The life history calendar may cover ten to fifteen pages, so it is cumbersome. An abbreviated version of the calendar, known as a time line, may be useful. For example, a person has a history of annual binge drinking during early October, with inevitable negative consequences (e.g., DUI one year, loss of job another). Early October is the anniversary of a car wreck that was his fault and killed his brother. A time line illustrates the repetition and supports the diagnosis of posttraumatic stress disorder subsequent to the car wreck.

Figure 6.6 expands the time frame of the case that is summarized in the sample life history calendar (Figure 6.4) and crystallizes the key themes that affected this young person's social and behavioral development. The loss of the attached relationships to his mother and grandmother, even though the family had been surrounded by instability, initiated a period of even more intense instability (including placement in repeatedly disrupted foster homes) and increasing severity of psychological problems. This excerpt from the time line depicts only up to age 14, so the major trauma had not yet occurred. These pre-trauma events help to explain why the young man's reaction to the tragedy was so severe.

Photographs and Other Artifacts

A social history file can begin to look like a scrapbook because many objects can be useful in explaining or illustrating key points about a person's life. Photos, certificates of accomplishment, artwork, poems, cards, and other objects offer information about life events. Photos might include not only the person but also other family members, a residence, a group of which the person was a part, and more. Letters or artwork created by the person can be particularly informative.

Tools to Describe Life Context

The social environmental context clearly influences human behavior. Social systems theory can explain how neighborhood and broader societal forces affect an individual, but systems theory is difficult for a typical layperson to follow. As the professional and person discuss the history, maps or charts help to explain the issues.

Geographic Maps

A few examples best illustrate how location may affect behavior.

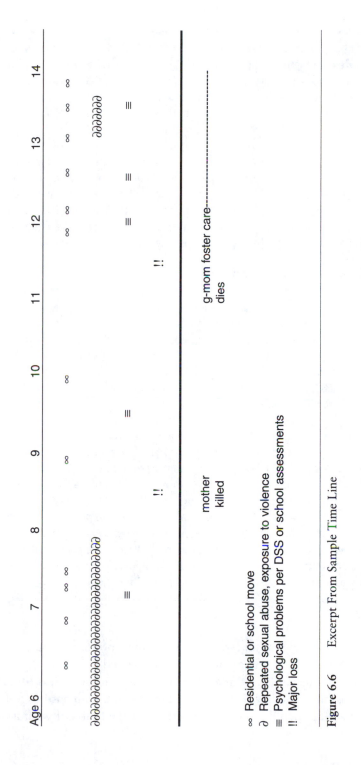

Figure 6.6 Excerpt From Sample Time Line

1. Marilyn was raised in a mill village in the 1950s, during a time when "town" residents, those with white-collar jobs, lived across town. The social expectation was that mill village kids would stay within the informal boundaries of their village, using only those parts of the town that catered to their needs. In her particular community, a railroad track created the boundary; she literally lived on the proverbial "other side of the tracks." For the first seventeen years of her life, she never left the village except to visit her grandparents on their farm twenty miles away. The village had strong social cohesion; residents felt comfortable there. When Marilyn married a "town boy," against his family's objections, and moved outside the village, she experienced anxiety and felt put down by those in her husband's social circle. She felt cut off from her family. A map of the town, showing where her family lived and where she lived after marriage, illustrates the distance and isolation.

2. Antonio, born in New York City to an unmarried mother with a drug addiction, was sent to live with his grandparents in South Carolina. Many of his mother's relatives lived in New York. Throughout his life, he moved often from New York to South Carolina and back, living for about six months to a year at each place, changing schools frequently. In each state, he lived with a variety of relatives, so his actual location changed. His was essentially a transient and unstable life. While he had many connections to relatives, he had no firmly attached relationships or caregivers. A map highlighted the various townships where he lived and the paths, with dates, that he took when traveling back and forth. The marking of the paths created an image that enriched the telling of the story about his unstable childhood.

3. Mark emigrated from Cambodia at age 7 with his family, who had been living in a squatter village. They were assisted by an Anglo religious congregation that found them a place to live in an "Asian" neighborhood. In the neighborhood, almost everyone was from Korea. Mark grew up feeling like a misfit. A few other Cambodian families lived in the area, but the relationships between Cambodians and Koreans were tenuous, and sometimes hostile. Given the geographic illiteracy of many Americans, showing a world map that illustrates how vastly physically distant Cambodia is from Korea helped to explain the cultural differences.

In each case, a map was an essential backdrop to promote people's comprehension of the facts and opinions being presented.

Not everyone has been trained to read a map, and some less educated people, possibly including jury members, may find a map hard to follow, so use of a map should begin with pointing out the basics of what a map illustrates, such as the boundaries, the legend, or the symbols on the map. Whenever possible, include generally familiar or famous sites on a map to ground the viewer.

Community Profile and Assessment

A community profile describes the key structural characteristics of a community, such as its boundaries, member characteristics, and governance structure. A community assessment goes beyond structural description to evaluate processes and opinions about the community.

Given that individuals tend to belong to several communities (i.e., those based in geography, experience, and interests), one or more community profiles or assessments may be useful as a social history assessment is conducted.

The Internet is an excellent source of community profiles. The place to start is the U.S. Census Bureau (http://www.census.gov/). GIS (geographic information) systems technology is so prevalent that even the smallest of towns has a Web site with its community profile.

Typically, a community profile will include the following:

- Geographic boundaries of the community
- Population (size, change over time, characteristics by age, race/ethnicity)
- History
- Governance
- Economic indicators (per capita income, household income, trend over time)
- Employment (occupations of residents, major industries, employment rates)
- Housing indicators (homeownership, median cost of housing units, average rent)
- Educational indicators

Community indicators are easier to interpret if they are presented in comparison with other locations. For example, the profile of one town may be presented with data for the county and state alongside. The relative advantage or disadvantage of the town will be more apparent.

Many communities also have assessment reports that are usually conducted in relation to a particular issue, such as assessing opportunities for economic development, health status, children's educational needs, homelessness, or other such topics. These assessment reports can be found on local Web sites such as those of the city or county government, United Way, regional planning councils, advocacy organizations, or government agencies.

The Community Tool Box (CTB; http://ctb.ku.edu/) offers an excellent guide to conducting a community assessment for purposes of community planning and action. The tools facilitate preparing basic profiles, determining issues of concern to the community, and assessing readiness for action. The CTB emphasizes social aspects of the community assessment process, noting that change happens through communication among key community members such as parents, religious leaders, school officials, leaders of tenants' associations, real estate agents, social service officials, law enforcement officers, advocates, and others. The tools can be useful for discovering information of utility in a social history assessment.

Several other valuable resources for conducting community assessments are available on the Internet, including these two:

- Asset-Based Community Development Institute (http://www.north-western.edu/IPR/abcd.html)
- Laboratory for Community and Economic Development at the University of Illinois (http://www.ag.uiuc.edu/~lced/)

An easy and common part of community assessment is the "windshield survey," which involves driving around, making notes, and possibly taking pictures. Observations are typically recorded about such factors as housing conditions (type, upkeep); road and sidewalk conditions; billboards or signs with information about the community; appearances of schools, churches, retail establishments, parks and other recreational facilities; and health care facilities. Observers also note what people are doing and how they interact.

Building Floor Plans and Other Drawings

Occasionally, drawing a floor plan can help bring to life a fact in the case. For example, George grew up in a strict, fundamental religious home. His father, a lay minister and carpenter, was a cruel disciplinarian. The father also had regular sexual relations with the oldest daughter in the family. He built a door that led from the back of the closet in the bedroom he shared with his wife to his daughter's bedroom. The boys in the home knew the door existed, because they could see it when they played in their sister's bedroom. Showing the room layouts, with notations of where everyone in the family slept, helped make the point to a prosecutor skeptical about pressing charges against the father.

In other cases, drawings can illustrate where children were locked in closets as punishment, or the distance from their room in the barn to the main house. If the facts call for clarification through a drawing, one should be made.

Ecological Chart

Figure 3.1, presented in Chapter 3, portrays the general ecological context of a family. Sometimes drawing the specific elements of a person's or family's ecosystem helps to enlighten the person and the historian regarding the specific resources and other influences that were present in the person's life. The person and the professional can fill out a set of concentric circles that identify individual, family, neighborhood, small group, organization, community-wide, and societal influences that are salient in the person's history.

Understanding a person's ecosystem can also shed light on the coping resources that have been available to the person. A community's resources indicate the capacity to protect and provide support. Absence of resources suggests capacity to induce harm or elicit negative behavior. Consider these two lives, figuratively summarized in Figure 6.7:

Sara Morris (not her real name), widowed 3 years ago when her husband was killed in a street fight, lives in an apartment complex with her two sons, ages 4 and 9. She works 29 hours a week as a sales clerk at a large bargain store. Her employer will not assign her more hours per week, so she is ineligible for benefits. She works a second job, up to 20 hours a week, at a convenience store. Her work hours vary each week. Sometimes she works until midnight. Her youngest child stays at a crowded day care facility that has no developmental programs but does provide good meals and a TV for the children to watch. Her oldest takes the bus to school and stays at home alone until Sara gets in from work. She pays teenagers in the neighborhood to stay with the boys when she works nights.

Ms. Morris usually keeps her doors locked and tries not to talk to the neighbors too much. She lives in an area where police are often called because of fights. She has been told that a house across from the apartment complex is a "crack house." The nearest bus stop is five blocks from the complex. Often she pays $5 a trip for a car ride to get groceries. The nearest church is nine blocks away. Ms. Morris has never been to a PTA meeting nor has she ever met her son's teachers. Ms. Morris feels exhausted most of the time and worried because her oldest son is failing in school and her youngest is so defiant.

Lasondra and
2 sons

Job, child care,
child support

Health care

Transportation

School, church

Parks, support
group, service

Figure 6.7 (Continued)

Lasondra Davis (not her real name) lives in an apartment complex with her two sons, ages 4 and 9. Ms. Davis, who has been divorced for 3 years, works at a bank from 7:30 am to 4:00 pm each day, with a half-hour for lunch. Through her job, she and her children get affordable health insurance and she can take sick leave when the children are ill. Her youngest child attends a Head Start program two blocks from her workplace. They ride the center van together each morning and evening. Her oldest takes the bus to and from school and stays at a neighbor's for after-school care.

On Saturday mornings Ms. Davis and her sons take the public bus to get groceries and run other errands. Each Wednesday a member of Ms. Davis' church gives her a ride to run errands before they attend family night activities together at the church. The boys' father pays financial child support through a court order, though they rarely see him. The boys are active in the city parks program, participating on team sports and often going to the recreation center, just three blocks from their complex, for activities. Ms. Davis attends neighborhood PTA meetings, sponsored by her son's school, at the center because she cannot get to the school at night; it is too far away. Twice a year a teacher or school social worker visits the Davis home.

Ms. Davis's family lives in another state. She and her sons regularly visit an elderly lady, Ms. Mary, who lives in their complex. The boys run the vacuum cleaner while Ms. Davis helps with chores. The boys love to sit with

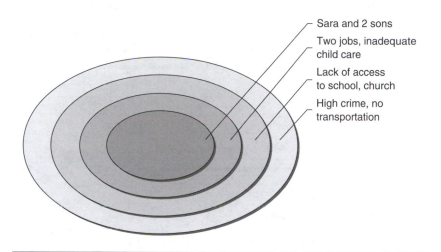

Sara and 2 sons

Two jobs, inadequate child care

Lack of access to school, church

High crime, no transportation

Figure 6.7   Comparison of Ecological Resources Available to Two Families

Ms. Mary and watch TV or read books. Each Monday evening Ms. Davis meets with other mothers of young children in a support group facilitated by a neighborhood family support program. Teenagers baby-sit while the mothers swap advice and listen to invited speakers from places like the health department or the extension service. Ms. Davis sometimes calls a support group member when she is feeling down.

Flextime, accessible and affordable day care, support from friends and neighbors, public transportation, effective court support, recreational facilities, family-friendly school programs, multiuse facilities, opportunities to show care, mutual support activities, public agency workers who go to where people are; families rely on resources like these. Somebody in the community—business manager, government officials, parents, churches, neighbors—planned these resources so families like the Davises could be supported. The Morris family is not so fortunate.

Knowing information like this about the ecological context of a social history sheds considerable light on how the person lived and learned to see the world.

Tools to Illustrate Case Theories

A picture can summarize complex theoretical information like no words can do.

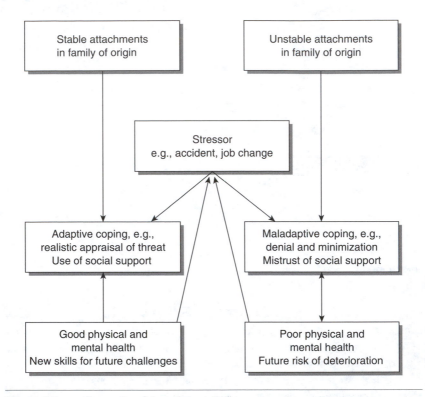

Figure 6.8   Synopsis of Attachment Influences on Stress Management

Figure 6.8 is a simple synopsis of a basic theory about the relationship of attachment to stress and its health consequences. The chart is useful in explaining to clients how stress and coping affects their lives and, over time, how repetitious coping habits can be harmful or helpful.

Figure 6.9, "Portrayal of Pathological Caregiving," is grounded in a particular case of a woman who developed physiological and psychological problems related to her caregiving for others. She did not feel unconditional affirmation or care from people around her and acquired a sense of self-worth by providing care at various times to a number of relatives in her extended care network. She gave child care to a nephew's two children for a while. She cared for a sister after major surgery. She nursed three different elderly relatives during their late stages of life. She responded to numerous requests for short-term assistance, even sitting for pets and tending plants while people were on vacation. Her pattern, though, was unhealthy for her. She worked herself to the point of exhaustion, refusing

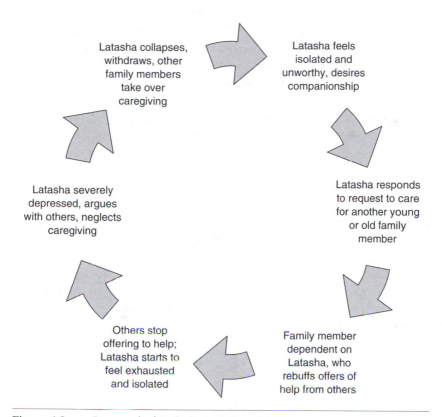

Latasha collapses, withdraws, other family members take over caregiving

Latasha feels isolated and unworthy, desires companionship

Latasha severely depressed, argues with others, neglects caregiving

Latasha responds to request to care for another young or old family member

Others stop offering to help; Latasha starts to feel exhausted and isolated

Family member dependent on Latasha, who rebuffs offers of help from others

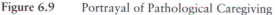

Figure 6.9   Portrayal of Pathological Caregiving

assistance from others, and had what some would call a need to be a "martyr." Her exhaustion led to stress-related gastrointestinal and heart problems. She could not seem to say "no" to requests, and so she would take to her bed with illness, offering a more "legitimate" excuse of incapacity. Once she regained her strength, she would again seek caregiving opportunities. Over time, this cycle was taking a major toll on her health.

Clients and others who have responsibility for client care often have keen insight when they develop a drawing or see a drawing the professional has developed. Visual aids are critical components of social history assessments.

Conclusion

A person's social life vibrates with energy, intricacy, and diversity. Even the person who sits quietly has social interactions with the surrounding world. To understand the life for purposes of self-enlightenment, making a record for posterity, or laying a foundation for change, tools can help to simplify that which is inherently complicated. History is essentially a form of communication. For one person to communicate with another, a clear mutual language is required. The social history assessment facilitated by a skilled professional can provide that language.

In a social history assessment, what starts as personal narrative is recorded descriptively and then interpretively. The fresh narration can be supplemented by visual aids and verbatim excerpts from the original narrative. The typical result is a document, a report that becomes a new part of the life history.

Note

1. The genograms in this chapter are drawn with Genogram-Maker Millennium v.1.1.0 (© 2001–2002, Sylvia Shellenberger, GenoWare, Macon, GA). A more advanced version of this software, known as GenoPro, is available at http://www.genopro.com

References

Adler, L. L. (2001). Women and gender roles. In L. L. Adler & U. P. Gielen (Eds.), *Cross-cultural topics in psychology* (pp. 103–114). Westport, CT: Praeger/Greenwood.

Ainsworth, M. D. S. (1989). Attachments beyond infancy. *American Psychologist, 44*(4), 709–716.

Amato, P. R. (1995). Single-parent households as settings for children's development, well-being, and attainment: A social network/resources perspective. *Sociological Studies of Children, 7,* 19–47.

American Academy of Pediatrics. (2006). *Media matters: A national media education campaign.* Retrieved April 26, 2006, from http://www.aap.org/advocacy/mmcamp.htm

American Psychiatric Association. (1994). *Diagnostic and statistical manual of mental disorders* (4th ed.). Washington, DC: Author.

American Psychological Association. (2003). *Ethical principles of psychologists and code of conduct.* Washington, DC: Author.

Anderson, N., Ones, D. S., Sinangil, H. K., & Viswesvaran, C. (Eds.). (2002). *Handbook of industrial, work, and organizational psychology: Vol. 2. Organizational psychology.* Thousand Oaks, CA: Sage.

Anderson, S. A., & Sabatelli, R. M. (1999). *Family interaction: A multigenerational developmental perspective.* Boston: Allyn & Bacon.

Andrews, A. B. (1997). Assessing neighbourhood and community factors that influence children's well-being. In A. Ben-Arieh & H. Wintersberger (Eds.), *Monitoring and measuring the state of children—Beyond survival* (pp. 127–141). Vienna, Austria: European Centre.

Andrews, A. B., & Kaufman, N. H. (Eds.). (1999). *Implementing the U.N. Convention on the Rights of the Child: A standard of living adequate for development.* Westport, CT: Praeger.

Artuerburn, S., & Felton. J. (2001). *Toxic faith.* Colorado Springs, CO: Shaw Publishers.

Atkinson, P., Coffey, A., Delamont, S., Lofland, J., & Lofland, L. (Eds.). (2001). *Handbook of ethnography.* Thousand Oaks, CA: Sage.

Atkinson, R. (1998). *The life story interview.* Thousand Oaks, CA: Sage.

Bandura, A. (1977). *Social learning theory.* Englewood Cliffs, NJ: Prentice Hall.

Bandura, A. (1997). *Self-efficacy: The exercise of control.* New York: W. H. Freeman.

Bandura, A. (2002). Social cognitive theory in cultural context. *Journal of Applied Psychology: An International Review, 51,* 269–290.

Barnett, W. S. (1995). Long-term effects of early childhood programs on cognitive and school outcomes. *Future of Children, 5*(3), 25–50.

Barone, T. (1995). Persuasive writings, vigilant readings, and reconstructed characters: The paradox of trust in educational storysharing. In J. A. Hatch & R. Wisniewski (Eds.), *Life history and narrative* (pp. 63–74). London: Falmer.

Bedrosian, R. C., & Bozicas, G. D. (1994). *Treating family of origin problems: A cognitive approach*. New York: Guilford.

Bem, S. L. (1993). *The lenses of gender: Transforming the debate on sexual inequality*. New Haven, CT: Yale University Press.

Bemak, F., & Greenberg, B. (1994). Southeast Asian refugee adolescents: Implications for counseling. *Journal of Multicultural Counseling and Development, 22*(2), 115–124.

Betancourt, H., & Lopez, S. R. (1993). The study of culture, ethnicity, and race in American psychology. *American Psychologist, 48*, 629–637.

Bernhardt, B., & Rauch, J. B. (1993). Genetic family histories: An aid to social work assessment. *Families in Society: The Journal of Contemporary Human Services, 74*(4), 195–206.

Bertalanffy, L. V. (1968). *General systems theory*. New York: George Braziller.

Biddell, T. R. (1997). Between nature and nurture: The role of human agency in the epigenesist of intelligence. In R. J. Sternberg (Ed.), *Intelligence, heredity, and environment* (pp. 193–242). New York: Cambridge University Press.

Bisman, C. D. (1999). Social work assessment: Case theory construction. *Families in Society: The Journal of Contemporary Human Services, 80*(3), 240–246.

Blumenfeld-Jones, D. (1995). Fidelity as a criterion for practicing and evaluating narrative inquiry. In J. A. Hatch & R. Wisniewski (Eds.), *Life history and narrative* (pp. 25–35). London: Falmer.

Bonham, V. L., Warshauer-Baker, E., & Collins, F. S. (2005). Race and ethnicity in the genome era: The complexity of the constructs. *American Psychologist, 60* (1), 9–15.

Booth, A., & Crouter, A. C. (1997). *Immigration and the family: Research and policy on U.S. immigrants.* Hillsdale, NJ: Lawrence Erlbaum.

Booth, L. (1991). *When God becomes a drug: Breaking the chains of religious addiction and abuse*. New York: Jeremy Tarcher/Putnam.

Bowen, M. (1985). *Family therapy in clinical practice*. Northvale, NJ: Jason Aronson.

Bowlby, J. (1969). *Attachment and loss: Vol. 1. Attachment*. New York: Basic Books.

Bowlby, J. (1973). *Attachment and loss: Vol. 2. Separation: Anxiety and anger*. New York: Basic Books.

Bowlby, J. (1980). *Attachment and loss: Vol. 3. Sadness and depression*. New York: Basic Books.

Branch, C. W. (1997). *Clinical interventions with gang adolescents and their families*. Boulder, CO: Westview.

Briere, J. N., & Elliott, D. N. (1994). Immediate and long-term impacts of child sexual abuse. *Future of Children, 4*(2), 54–69.

Bronfenbrenner, U. (1999). Environments in developmental perspective: Theoretical and operational models. In S. L. Friedman & T. D. Wachs (Eds.), *Measuring environment across the life span: Emerging methods and concepts* (pp. 3–28). Washington, DC: American Psychological Association.

Bronfenbrenner, U. (2005a). The bioecological theory of human development. In U. Bronfenbrenner (Ed.), *Making human beings human: Bioecological perspectives on human development* (pp. 3–15). Thousand Oaks, CA: Sage.

Bronfenbrenner, U. (2005b). Ecological systems theory. In U. Bronfenbrenner (Ed.), *Making human beings human: Bioecological perspectives on human development* (pp. 106–173). Thousand Oaks, CA: Sage.

Brooks-Gunn, J., Duncan, G. J., & Aber, L. J. (Eds.). (1997). *Neighborhood poverty: Vol. 1. Context and consequences for children.* New York: Russell Sage.

Brooks-Gunn, J., Klebanov, P. K., & Liaw, F. (1995). The learning, physical, and emotional environment of the home in the context of poverty: The Infant Health and Development Program. *Children and Youth Services Review, 17*(1/2), 251–276.

Bruce, E. J., & Schultz, C. L. (2001). *Nonfinite loss and grief: A psychoeducational approach.* Baltimore: Paul H. Brookes.

Bruner, E. M. (1984). The opening up of anthropology. In E. M. Bruner (Ed.), *Text, play, and story: The construction and reconstruction of self and society* (pp. 1–18). Washington, DC: American Ethnological Society.

Bruner, J. (1986). *Actual minds, possible worlds.* Cambridge, MA: Harvard University Press.

Brysk, A. (Ed.). (2002). *Globalization and human rights.* Berkeley and Los Angeles: University of California Press.

Burnett, A., & Thompson, K. (2005). Enhancing the psychosocial well-being of asylum seekers and refugees. In K. H. Barrett & W. H. George (Eds.), *Race, culture, psychology, and law* (pp. 205–224). Thousand Oaks, CA: Sage.

Buzawa, E. S., & Buzawa, C. G. (Eds.). (1996). *Do arrests and restraining orders work?* Thousand Oaks, CA: Sage.

Canda, E. R. (1998). *Spirituality in social work.* Binghamton, NY: Haworth.

Carnes, P. J. (1997). *The betrayal bond.* Deerfield, FL: Health Communications.

Caspi, A., Moffit, T. F., Thornton, A., Freedman, D., Amell, J. W., Barrington, H., Smeijers, J., & Silva, P. A. (1996). The life history calendar: A research and clinical assessment method for collecting retrospective event-history data. *International Journal of Methods in Psychiatric Research, 6,* 101–114.

Catalano, R. F., Berglund, M. L., Ryan, J. A. M., Lonczak, H. S., & Hawkins, J. D. (2004). Positive youth development in the United States: Research findings on evaluations of positive youth development programs. In C. Peterson (Ed.), Positive youth development: Realizing the potential of youth [Special issue]. *Annals of the American Academy of Political and Social Science, 591,* 98–124.

Catherill, D. R. (2004). *The handbook of stress, trauma, and the family.* London: Brunner-Routledge.

Centers for Disease Control, National Institute for Occupational Health and Safety. *Organization of work: Measurement tools for research and practice.* Retrieved May 6, 2006, from http://www2a.cdc.gov/nioshworkorg/detail .asp?id=85

Child Trends DataBank. (2005). *Child Care Indicators.* Retrieved July 26, 2005, from http://www.childtrendsdatabank.org/indicators/21ChildCare.cfm

Coleman, J. C. (1988). Social capital in the creation of human capital. *American Journal of Sociology, 94,* 95–120.

Coles, R. (1990). *The spiritual life of children*. Boston: Houghton Mifflin.

Collins, F. S., Green, E. D., Guttmacher, A. E., & Guyer, M. S. (2003). A vision for the future of genomics research. *Nature, 422*, 835–847.

Collins, N. L., Guichard, A. C., & Ford, M. B. (2004). Working models of attachment: New developments and emerging themes. In W. S. Rholes & J. A. Simpson (Eds.), *Adult attachment: Theory, research, and clinical implications* (pp. 196–239). New York: Guilford.

Community Tool Box. (2006). Retrieved April 26, 2006, from http://ctb.ku.edu

Connell, R. (1995). *Masculinities*. Cambridge, UK: Polity.

Corcoran, M. (1995). Rags to riches: Poverty and mobility in the United States. *Annual Review of Sociology, 21*, 237–267.

Cormier, S., & Cormier, W. H. (1996). *Interviewing strategies for helpers: Fundamental skills and cognitive behavioral interventions* (4th ed.). Belmont, CA: Brooks/Cole.

Coupland, S., Serovich, J., & Glenn, J. (1995). Reliability in constructing genograms: A study among marriage and family therapy doctoral students. *Journal of Marital and Family Therapy, 21*(3), 251–263.

Cox, R. P., Keltner, N., & Hogan, B. (2003). Family assessment tools. In R. P. Cox, *Health related counseling with families of diverse cultures: Family, health, and cultural competencies* (pp. 145–167). Westport, CT: Greenwood.

Coyne, J. C., & Downey, G. (1991). Social factors and psychopathology: Stress, social support, and coping processes. *Annual Review of Psychology, 42*, 401–425.

Creswell, J. W. (2002). *Research design: Qualitative, quantitative, and mixed method approaches*. Thousand Oaks, CA: Sage.

D'Andrade, R. G., & Strauss, C. (Eds.). (1992). *Human motives and cultural models*. Cambridge, UK: Cambridge University Press.

deGraaf, J., Wann, D., & Naylor, T. H. (2001). *Affluenza: The all-consuming epidemic*. Williston, VT: Berrett-Koehler.

DeMaria, R., Weeks, G., & Hof, L. (1999). *Focused genograms: Intergenerational assessment of individuals, couples, and families*. New York: Brunner/Mazel.

Denzin, N. K. (1989). *Interpretive biography*. Newbury Park, CA: Sage.

DiLalla, L. F. (2002). Behavior genetics of aggression in children: Review and future directions. *Developmental Review, 22*, 593–622.

Dodge, K. A., Bates, J. E., & Pettit, G. S. (1990). Mechanisms in the cycle of violence. *Science, 250*, 1678–1683.

Donahey, K. M. (2004). *Sexual health concerns: Interviewing and history taking for health practitioners* (2nd ed.). Dordrecht, The Netherlands: Kluwer Academic.

Drake, P., & Sherrill, B. (2004). *Missing pieces: How to find birth parents and adopted children—A search and reunion guidebook*. Westminster, MD: Heritage Books.

Dugan, T., & Coles, R. (Eds.). (1989). *The child in our times: Studies in the development of resiliency*. New York: Brunner/Mazel.

Duncan, C. (1996). Understanding persistent poverty: Social class context in rural communities. *Rural Sociology, 61*(1), 103–124.

Duncan, G. J., & Brooks-Gunn, J. (1997). Income effects across the life span: Integration and interpretation. In G. J. Duncan & J. Brooks-Gunn (Eds.), *Consequences of growing up poor* (pp. 596–610). New York: Russell Sage.

Duncan, G. J., Yeung, W. J., Brooks-Gunn, J., & Smith, J. R. (1998). How much does childhood poverty affect the life chances of children? *American Sociological Review, 63*, 406–423.

Duncan, T. E., Duncan, S. C., & Okut, H. (2003). A multilevel contextual model of neighborhood collective efficacy. *American Journal of Community Psychology, 32*(3–4), 245–252.

Earls, F. (1999). Frontiers of research on children, youth and families. *Journal of Community Psychology, 27*, 517–524.

Earls, F., & Buka, S. (2000). Measurement of community characteristics. In S. Meisels & J. Shonkoff (Eds.), *Handbook of early childhood intervention* (2nd ed., pp. 309–324). Cambridge, UK: Cambridge University Press.

Easterlin, R. A. (2000). Income and happiness: Towards a unified theory. *Economic Journal, 111*, 465–484.

Eckenrode, J., Rowe, E., Laird, M., & Brathwaite, J. (1995). Mobility as a mediator of the effects of child maltreatment on academic performance. *Child Development, 66*, 1130–1142.

Eisenberg, N., Fabes, R. A., Guthrie, I. K., & Reiser, M. (2001). The role of emotionality and regulation in children's social competence and adjustment. In L. Pulkkinen & A. Caspi (Eds.), *Paths to successful development: Personality in the life course* (pp. 46–70). Cambridge, UK: Cambridge University Press.

Elder, G. H. (1994). Time, human agency, and social change: Perspectives on life course. *Social Psychology Quarterly, 57*(1), 4–15.

Erdman, H. P., & Foster, S. W. (1986). Computer-assisted assessment with couples and families. *Family Therapy, 13*(1), 23–40.

Evans, G. W. (1999). Measurement of the physical environment as stressor. In S. L. Friedman & T. D. Wachs (Eds.), *Measuring environment across the life span: Emerging methods and concepts* (pp. 249–277). Washington, DC: American Psychological Association.

Families and Work Institute. (n.d.). Retrieved April 16, 2006, from http://www.familiesandwork.org

Feingold, A. (1992). Gender differences in mate selection preferences: A test of the parental investment model. *Psychological Bulletin, 112*(1), 125–139.

Fields, J., & Casper, L. M. (2001). *America's families and living arrangements: Population characteristics, 2000.* Washington, DC: U.S. Bureau of the Census, P20–537.

Freud, A., & Burlingham, D. (1944). *Infants without families: The case for and against residential nurseries.* New York: International University Press.

Furstenberg, F. F., Eccles, J., & Cook, T. D. (1999). *Managing to make it: Urban families and adolescent success.* Chicago: University of Chicago Press.

Garbarino, J. (1997). *Raising children in a socially toxic environment.* San Francisco: Jossey-Bass.

Garmezy, N. (1985). Stress resistant children: The search for protective factors. In J. Stevenson (Ed.), *Recent research in developmental psychopathology* (pp. 213–233). Oxford, UK: Pergamon.

Garmezy, N. (1991). Resiliency and vulnerability to adverse developmental outcomes associated with poverty. *American Behavioral Scientist, 34*, 416–430.

Garner, C. L., & Raudenbush, S. W. (1991). Neighborhood effects on educational attainment: A multilevel analysis. *Sociology of Education, 64*, 251–262.

Garnets, L. D., & Peplau, L. A. (2000). Understanding women's sexualities and sexual orientations: An introduction. *Journal of Social Issues, 56*(2), 181–192.

Gelles, R. J. (1993). Constraints against family violence: How well do they work? *American Behavioral Scientist, 36*(5), 575–586.

George, L. K., Ellison, C. G., & Larson, D. B. (2002). Explaining the relationships between religious involvement and health. *Psychological Inquiry, 13*(3), 190–200.

Gephart, M. A. (1997). Neighborhoods and communities as contexts for development. In J. Brooks-Gunn, G. J. Duncan, & J. L. Aber (Eds.), *Neighborhood poverty: Vol. 1. Context and consequences for children* (pp. 1–43). New York: Russell Sage.

Gephart, M. A., & Brooks-Gunn, J. (1997). Introduction. In J. Brooks-Gunn, G. J. Duncan, & L. J. Aber (Eds.), *Neighborhood poverty: Vol. 1. Context and consequences for children* (pp. xiii–xxii). New York: Russell Sage.

Germain, C. B. (1991). *Human behavior in the social environment: An ecological view*. New York: Columbia University Press.

Gerson, R. (1995). The family life cycle: Phases, stages, and crises. In R. H. Mikesell, D. Lusterman, & S. H. McDaniel (Eds.), *Integrating family therapy: Handbook of family psychology and systems theory* (pp. 91–111). Washington, DC: American Psychological Association.

Giele, J. Z. (1998). Innovation in the typical life course. In J. Z. Giele & G. H. Elder (Eds.), *Methods of life course research: Qualitative and quantitative approaches* (pp. 231–263). Thousand Oaks, CA: Sage.

Giele, J. Z., & Elder, G. H. (Eds.). (1998). *Methods of life course research: Qualitative and quantitative approaches*. Thousand Oaks, CA: Sage.

Goodson, I. F. (1995). The story so far: Personal knowledge and the political. In J. A. Hatch & R. Wisniewski (Eds.), *Life history and narrative* (pp. 89–98). London: Falmer.

Gross, J. J. (1998). Sharpening the focus: Emotional regulation, arousal, and social competence. *Psychological Inquiry, 9*(4), 287–290.

Groth-Marnat, G. (1997). *Handbook of psychological assessment* (3rd ed.). New York: John Wiley.

Gutierrez, L. M., Parsons, R. J., & Cox, E. O. (1998). *Empowerment in social work practice: A sourcebook*. Pacific Grove, CA: Brooks/Cole.

Hagan, J., MacMillan, R., & Wheaton, B. (1996). New kid in town: Social capital and the life course effects of family migration on children. *American Sociological Review, 61*, 368–385.

Haines, V. A., Beggs, J. J., & Hurlbert, J. S. (2002). Exploring the structural contexts of the support process: Social networks, social statuses, social support, and psychological distress. *Social Networks and Health, 8*, 269–292.

Hamburg, D. A. (1996). *A developmental strategy to prevent lifelong damage*. New York: Carnegie Corporation of New York.

Hannerz, U. (2000). Scenarios for peripheral cultures. In F. J. Lechner & J. Boli (Eds.), *The globalization reader* (pp. 331–337). Malden, MA: Blackwell.

Hartman, A. (1995). Diagrammatic assessment of family relationships. *Families in Society, 76*(2), 111–122.

Hatch, J. A., & Wisniewski, R. (Eds.). (1995). *Life history and narrative.* London: Falmer.

Henry, B., Moffitt, T. E., Caspi, A., Langley, J., & Silva, P. A. (1994). On the "remembrance" of things past: A longitudinal evaluation of the retrospective method. *Psychological Assessment, 6,* 92–101.

Hetherington, E. M., & Clingempeel, W. G. (1992). Coping with marital transitions. *Monographs of the Society for Research in Child Development, 57* (Serial Nos. 2–3).

Heyl, B. S. (2001). Ethnographic interviewing. In P. Atkinson, A. Coffey, S. Delamont, J. Lofland, & L. Lofland (Eds.), *Handbook of ethnography,* (pp. 369–383). Thousand Oaks, CA: Sage.

Hopper, J. (2006). *Sexual abuse of males: Prevalence, possible lasting effects, and resources.* Retrieved July 13, 2006, from http://www.jimhopper.com/male-ab/

Howe, Mark L. (2000). *The fate of early memories: Developmental science and the retention of childhood experiences.* Cambridge: MIT Press.

Hyde, J. S., & Jaffe, S. R. (2000). Becoming a heterosexual adult: The experiences of young women. *Journal of Social Issues, 56*(2), 283–296.

Janoff-Bulman, R. (1992). *Shattered assumptions: Towards a new psychology of trauma.* New York: Free Press.

Josselson, R., & Lieblich, A. (Eds.). (1993). *The narrative study of lives: Vol. 1.* Newbury Park, CA: Sage.

Josselson, R., & Lieblich, A. (Eds.). (1995). *The narrative study of lives: Vol. 3.* Thousand Oaks, CA: Sage.

Kagan, R., & Schlosberg, S. (1989). *Families in perpetual crisis.* New York: W. W. Norton.

Kaplan, L., & Girard, J. L. (1994). *Strengthening high-risk families: A handbook for practitioners.* New York: Maxwell Macmillan International.

Kellam, S. G., Ling, X., Merisca, R., Brown, C. H., & Ialongo, N. (1998). The effect of the level of aggression in the first grade classroom on the course and malleability of aggressive behavior into middle school. *Development and Psychopathology, 10,* 165–185.

King, D. (1999). *Get the facts on anyone* (3rd ed.). New York: Macmillan.

Kirby, L. D., & Fraser, M. W. (1997). Risk and resilience in childhood. In M. W. Fraser (Ed.), *Risk and resilience in childhood: An ecological perspective* (pp. 10–33). Washington, DC: NASW Press.

Kite, M. E. (2001). Changing times, changing gender roles: What do we want women and men to be? In R. K. Unger (Ed.), *Handbook of the psychology of women and gender* (pp. 215–227). New York: John Wiley.

Kobasa, S. (1985). Stressful life events, personality, and health: An inquiry into hardiness. In A. Monat & R. Lazarus (Eds.), *Stress and coping* (2nd ed., pp. 174–191). New York: Columbia University Press.

Kretzmann, P., & McKnight, J. L. (1993). *Building communities from the inside out.* Evanston, IL: Northwestern University, Asset-Based Community Development Institute.

Kuehl, B. P. (1995). The solution-oriented genogram: A collaborative approach. *Journal of Marital and Family Therapy, 21,* 239–250.

Kvale, S. (1996). *Interviews: An introduction to qualitative research interviewing.* Thousand Oaks, CA; Sage.

Laumann, E. O., Gagnon, J. H., Michael, R. T., & Michaels, S. (1994). *The social organization of sexuality: Sexual practices in the United States.* Chicago: University of Chicago Press.

Lazarus, R. S. (2000). Toward better research on stress and coping. *American Psychologist, 55*(6), 665–673.

Leiblum, S. R., & Rosen, R. C. (Eds.). (1988). *Sexual desire disorders.* New York: Guilford.

Lerner, M. (1991). *Surplus powerlessness: The psychodynamics of everyday life . . . and the psychology of individual and social transformation.* Atlantic Highlands, NJ: Humanities Press International.

Leventhal, T., & Brooks-Gunn, J. (2000). The neighborhoods they live in: The effects of neighborhood residence on child and adolescent outcomes. *Psychological Bulletin, 126*(2), 309–337.

Lieblich, A., Tuvel-Mashiach, R., & Zilber, T. (1998). *Narrative research: Reading, analysis, and interpretation.* Thousand Oaks, CA: Sage.

Lindahl, R. (2006). *The role of organizational climate and culture in the school improvement process: A review of the knowledge base.* Retrieved May 6, 2006, from http://cnx.org/content/m13465/latest/

Little, P. M. D., & Harris, E. (2003). *A review of Out-of-School Time program quasi-experimental and experimental evaluation results* (Out- of-School Time Evaluation Snapshot No. 1). Retrieved July 11, 2006, from Harvard Family Research Project at http://www.gse.harvard.edu/hfrp/projects/afterschool/resources/snapshot1.html

Loftus, E. F. (1993). The reality of repressed memories. *American Psychologist, 48,* 518–537.

LTC Info. (2003). *The market for long-term care.* Retrieved November 19, 2003, from http://www.ltc-info.com/market.html

Luhmann, N. (1995). *Social systems.* Stanford, CA: Stanford University Press.

MacBeth, T. (Ed.). (1996). *Tuning in to young viewers.* Newbury Park, CA: Sage.

Mack, J. E. (1994). Power, powerlessness, and empowerment in psychotherapy. *Psychiatry: Interpersonal and biological processes, 57*(2), 178–198.

Martin, E. P., & Martin, J. M. (2003). *Spirituality and the Black helping tradition in social work.* Washington, DC: National Association of Social Workers.

McCubbin, H., McCubbin, M., Thompson, E., & Fromer, J. (Eds.). (1995). *Resilience in ethnic minority families: Vol. 1. Native and immigrant families.* Madison: University of Wisconsin, Center for Excellence in Family Studies.

McCubbin, H., McCubbin, M., McCubbin, A., & Futrell, J. (Eds.). (1995). *Resilience in ethnic minority families: Vol. 2. African-American families.* Madison: University of Wisconsin, Center for Excellence in Family Studies.

McGeer, V. (2004). The art of good hope. *Annals of the American Academy of Political and Social Science, 592,* 100–127.

McGoldrick, M., Gerson, R., & Shellenberger, S. (1999). *Genograms: Assessment and intervention* (2nd ed.). New York: W. W. Norton.

McLoyd, V. C. (1998). Socioeconomic disadvantage and child development. *American Psychologist, 53,* 185–204.

Meyers, J. E. B., Berliner, L., Briere, J., Hendrix, C. T., Jenny, S., & Reid, T. (Eds.). (2002). *The APSAC handbook on child maltreatment* (2nd ed.). Thousand Oaks, CA: Sage.

Miller, B. A. (2005). Intergenerational transmission of religiousness and spirituality. In W. R. Miller & H. D. Delaney (Eds.), *Judeo-Christian perspectives on psychology* (pp. 227–244). Washington, DC: American Psychological Association.

Minuchin, P., Colapinto, J., & Minuchin, S. (1998). *Working with families of the poor*. New York: Guilford.

Moore, K., Vandivere, S., & Ehrle, J. (2000). *Assessing turbulence and child well-being* (Report: New Federalism Policy Brief B-18). Washington, DC: Child Trends.

Morrison, J. (1993). *The first interview: A guide for clinicians*. New York: Guilford.

Mortimer, J. T., & Shanahan, M. J. (Eds.). (2003). *Handbook of the life course*. New York: Plenum.

Myers, J. E. B. (1998). *Legal issues in child abuse and neglect practice*. Thousand Oaks, CA: Sage.

National Association of Social Workers. (1999). *Code of ethics*. Washington, DC: Author.

National Endowment for the Humanities. (1999). *My history is America's history*. Washington, DC: Author.

Orpinas, P., & Horne, A. M. (2006). *Bullying prevention: Creating a positive school climate and developing social competence*. Washington, DC: American Psychological Association.

Pallone, N. J. (Ed.). (2003). *Love, romance, sexual interaction: Research perspectives from current psychology*. New Brunswick, NJ: Transaction Publishers.

Patterson, G. (1982). *Coercive family process*. Eugene, OR: Castalia.

Peacock, J. L., & Holland, D. C. (1993). The narrated self: Life stories in process. *Ethos, 21*(4), 367–383.

Peplau, L. A., & Garnets, L. D. (2000). A new paradigm for understanding women's sexuality and orientation. *Journal of Social Issues, 56*(2), 329–350.

Philpot, C. L., Brooks, G., Lusterman, D.-D., & Nutt, R. (Eds.). (1997). *Bridging separate gender worlds*. Washington, DC: American Psychological Association.

Plomin, R., & Daniels, D. (1987). Why are children in the same family so different from one another? *Behavioral and Brain Sciences, 14,* 373–427.

Plomin, R., DeFries, J. C., & McClearn, G. E. (1990). *Behavioral genetics: A primer* (2nd ed.). New York: W. H. Freeman.

Plummer, K. (2001). The call of life stories in ethnographic research. In P. Atkinson, A. Coffey, S. Delamont, J. Lofland, & L. Lofland (Eds.), *Handbook of ethnography* (pp. 395–406). Thousand Oaks, CA: Sage.

Poelmans, S. A. Y. (Ed.). (2005). *Work and family: An international perspective*. Mahwah, NJ: Lawrence Erlbaum.

Reed-Danahay, D. (2001). Autobiography, intimacy, and ethnography. In P. Atkinson, A. Coffey, S. Delamont, J. Lofland, & L. Lofland (Eds.), *Handbook of ethnography* (pp. 407–425). Thousand Oaks, CA: Sage.

Reid, J. B., Patterson, G. R., & Snyder, J. (2002). *Antisocial behavior in children and adolescents: A developmental analysis and model for intervention.* Washington, DC: American Psychological Association.

Rhode Island Kids Count. (2005). *Getting ready: Findings from the National School Readiness Indicators Initiative: A 17-state partnership.* Retrieved July 18, 2006, from http://www.gettingready.org/matriarch/

Richmond, M. (1917). *Social diagnosis.* New York: Russell Sage.

Rogers, R. (Ed.). (1997). *Clinical assessment of malingering and deception* (2nd ed.). New York: Guilford.

Rohrbaugh, M., Rogers, J., & McGoldrick, M. (1992). How do experts read family genograms? *Family Systems Medicine, 10*(1), 79–89.

Rosen, A. (Ed.). (2005). *Frozen dreams: Psychodynamic dimensions of infertility and assisted reproduction.* Hillsdale, NJ: Analytic Press.

Rothblum, E. D. (2000). Sexual orientation and sex in women's lives: Conceptual and methodological issues. *Journal of Social Issues, 56*(2), 193–204.

Rotter, J. B. (1982). *The development and application of social learning theory.* New York: Praeger.

Rutter, M. (1987). Psychosocial resilience and protective mechanisms. *American Journal of Orthopsychiatry, 57*(3), 316–331.

Sampson, R. J. (2000). A neighborhood-level perspective on social change and the social control of adolescent delinquency. In L. J. Crockett & R. K. Silbereisen (Eds.), *Negotiating adolescence in times of social change* (pp. 178–188). New York: Cambridge University Press.

Santisteban, D. A. (2002). Integrating the study of ethnic culture and family psychology intervention science. In H. A. Liddle, D. A. Santisteban, R. F. Levant, & J. H. Bray (Eds.), *Family psychology: Science-based interventions* (pp. 331–351). Washington, DC: American Psychological Association.

Satow, R. (Ed.). (2001). *Gender and social life.* Needham Heights, MA: Allyn & Bacon.

Sattler, J. M. (1992). *Assessment of children* (3rd ed.). San Diego: Jerome M. Sattler.

Schneider, B., & Smith, D. B. (Eds.). (2004). *Personality and organizations.* Mahwah, NJ: Lawrence Erlbaum.

Schoon, I., Bynner, J., Joshi, H., Parsons, S., Wiggins, R. D., & Sacker, A. (2002). The influence of context, timing, and duration of risk experiences for the passage from childhood to midadulthood. *Child Development, 73*(5), 1486–1504.

See, L. A. (Ed.). (1998). *Human behavior in the social environment from an African American perspective.* New York: Haworth.

Seidman, E., Aber, J. L., & French, S. E. (2004). The organization of schooling and adolescent development. In K. I. Maton, C. J. Schellenbach, B. J. Leadbeater, & A. L. Solarz (Eds.), *Investing in children, youth, families, and communities: Strengths-based research and policy* (pp. 233–250). Washington, DC: American Psychological Association.

Seligman, M. (1995). *The optimistic child.* Boston: Houghton Mifflin.

Shonkoff, J. P., & Phillips, D. A. (Eds.). (2000). *From neurons to neighborhoods: The science of early childhood development.* Washington, DC: National Academy Press.

Simeonsson, R. (1995). *Risk, resilience, and prevention: Promoting the well-being of all children.* Baltimore: Paul H. Brookes.

Sirotnak, A. P. (2003, March 14). Child abuse and neglect: Failure to thrive. *EMedicine Journal, 4*(3). Retrieved July 18, 2006, from the emedicine Web site, http://www.emedicine.com/

Skelton, J. R., & Matthews, P. M. (2001). Teaching sexual history taking to health care professionals in primary care. *Medical Education, 35*(6), 603–609.

Smedley, A., & Smedley, B. D. (2005). Race as biology is fiction, racism as a social problem is real: Anthropological and historical perspectives on the social construction of race. *American Psychologist, 60*(1), 16–26.

Snyder, D. K., Cavell, T. A., Heffer, R. W., & Mangrum, L. F. (1995). Marital and family assessment: A multifaceted, multilevel approach. In R. H. Mikesell, D. Lusterman, & S. H. McDaniel (Eds.), *Integrating family therapy: Handbook of family psychology and systems theory* (pp. 163–182). Washington, DC: American Psychological Association.

Snyder, D. K., Cozzi, J. J., & Mangrum, L. F. (2002). Conceptual issues in assessing couples and families. In H. A. Liddle, D. A. Santisteban, R. F. Levant, & J. H. Bray (Eds.), *Family psychology: Science-based interventions* (pp. 69–87). Washington, DC: American Psychological Association.

Starnes, J. L. (2002). *How to select a qualified and credible private investigator.* Retrieved July 31, 2005, from the Expert Law Web site at http://www.expertlaw.com/library/investigators/hiring_investigators.html

Stern, A. (2000). *Everything starts from prayer: Mother Teresa's meditations on spiritual life for people of all faiths.* Ashland, OR: White Cloud.

Strauss, A., & Corbin, J. (1998). *Basics of qualitative research: Techniques and procedures for developing grounded theory.* Thousand Oaks, CA: Sage.

Super, C. M., & Harkness, S. (1999). The environment as culture in developmental research. In S. L. Friedman & T. D. Wachs (Eds.), *Measuring environment across the life span: Emerging methods and concepts* (pp. 279–323). Washington, DC: American Psychological Association Press.

Sussman, M. B., Steinmetz, S. K., & Peterson, G. W. (Eds.). (1999). *Handbook of marriage and the family* (2nd ed.). New York: Plenum.

Tamis-LaMonda, C. S., & Cabrera, N. (2002). *Handbook of father involvement: Multidisciplinary perspectives.* Mahwah, NJ: Lawrence Erlbaum.

Thompson, R. A. (1998). Empathy and its origins in early development. In S. Braten (Ed.), *Intersubjective communication and emotion in early ontology* (pp. 144–157). Cambridge, UK: Cambridge University Press.

Tremblay, C., Herbert, M., & Piche, C. (1999). Coping strategies and social support as mediators of consequences in child sexual abuse victims. *Child Abuse & Neglect, 23,* 929–945.

Tucker, C., Marx, J., & Long, L. (1998). "Moving on": Residential mobility and children's school lives. *Sociology of Education, 71,* 111–129.

United Nations. (1994). *Guide for a national action programme on the International Year of the Family.* New York: Author.

Van der Kolk, B. A., McFarlane, A. C., & Weisaeth, L. (Eds.). (1996). *Traumatic stress: The effects of overwhelming experience on mind, body, and society.* New York: Guilford.

Vannoy, D., & Dubeck, P. J. (Eds.). (1998). *Challenges for work and family in the 21st century.* New York: Aldine de Gruyter.

Walsh, F. (1998). *Strengthening family resilience.* New York: Guilford.

Walsh, F., & McGoldrick, M. (Eds.). (1991). *Living beyond loss: Death in the family.* New York: W. W. Norton.

Walton, E., & Smith, C. (1999). The genogram: A tool for assessment and intervention in child welfare. *Journal of Family Social Work, 3*(3), 3–20.

Watson, C. B., Chemers, M. M., & Preiser, N. (2001). Collective efficacy: A multilevel analysis. *Personality & Social Psychology Bulletin, 27*(8), 1057–1068.

Watson, J. (2002). Taking a sexual history. In D. Miller & J. Green (Eds.), *Psychology of sexual health* (pp. 115–124). Oxford, UK: Blackwell Science.

Watts, C., & Shrader, E. (1998). The genogram: A new research tool to document patterns of decision-making, conflict and vulnerability within households. *Health Policy Planning, 13*(4), 459–464.

Weatherall, A., Gavey, N., & Potts, A. (2002). So whose words are they anyway? *Feminism & Psychology, 12*(4), 531–539.

Webb, N. B. (2002). *Helping bereaved children: A handbook for practitioners* (2nd ed.). New York: Guilford.

Weiner, V. (1999). *Winning the war against youth gangs: A guide for teens, families, and communities.* Westport, CT: Greenwood.

Wetherell, M. (1996). Life histories/Social histories. In M. Wetherell (Ed.), *Identities, groups, and social issues* (pp. 300–361). London: Sage.

Williams, J. (2000). *Unbending gender: Why family and work conflict and what to do about it.* New York: Oxford University Press.

Zilbergeld, B. (1992). *The new male sexuality.* New York: Bantam.

Index

About the Author

Arlene Bowers Andrews, PhD, LISW, community psychologist and Professor of Social Work at the University of South Carolina, has extensive experience in community-based practice and research, program evaluation, and services systems for families affected by turbulence. At USC, she was a founder and former director of the Institute for Families in Society, an interdisciplinary research center that conducts research to enhance families through community partnerships. Prior to her academic career, she was the founding executive director of Sistercare, a multi-county system of services to families affected by intimate partner violence, founding executive director of Prevent Child Abuse–South Carolina, and a board member of multiple community and regional organizations, including the Southern Regional Council. She served for 8 years on the South Carolina Joint Legislative Committee on Children and Families and is an active volunteer in faith-based youth development work. She has been an expert witness on matters of family history and human behavior in federal and several state courts.

She is coeditor of *Implementing the UN Convention on the Rights of the Child: A Standard of Living Adequate for Development* (1999), co-author with Elizabeth Beck and Sarah Escholz of *In the Shadow of Death: Families of Loved Ones Who Face the Death Penalty* (2006), and author of *Victimization and Survivor Services* (1992), *Send Me! The Story of Salkehatchie Summer Service* (2006), and several articles and book chapters regarding violence prevention and community systems development.

Dr. Andrews is a graduate of Duke University and the University of South Carolina.